SHE

AUTHOR

Harriet Hall is a London-based journalist with an expertise in feminism and fashion history. Currently Head of Digital Features at *Stylist* magazine, where she presents and produces videos, conducts celebrity and political interviews and edits the reputable 'Ask a Feminist' column, Harriet also works as a broadcaster, appearing on the BBC, Sky News, BBC Radio 4 *Woman's Hour* and Talk Radio, as well as speaking widely at panel events. She has also held positions at BBC News Channel, *Marie Claire* and *InStyle* magazine. When she's not dismantling the patriarchy, Harriet can be found curating her wardrobe or wandering the halls of museums.

Find Harriet on Twitter @Harri_Grace and Instagram @harri.grace

ILLUSTRATOR

Alice Skinner is best known for her satirical drawings, often tackling political issues with a sense of humour. She is based in London where she graduated with a degree in illustration last year. Since then she has been establishing her freelance career as well as setting up her own greeting card line. Her recent body of work sees her reimagining classical art from the likes of Picasso for the social media generation, pairing the illustrations with meme-inspired captions which she shares on her ever growing Instagram page.

Find Alice on Instagram @thisisaliceskinner

SHE

*A Celebration of
Renegade Women*

HARRIET HALL

With illustrations by Alice Skinner

First published in 2018 by
HEADLINE HOME
An imprint of HEADLINE PUBLISHING GROUP

1

Cataloguing in Publication Data is available from the British Library

ISBN 978 1 4722 4985 2

Typeset in Versailles 9.75/15.25 by Jouve (UK), Milton Keynes

Printed and bound in Great Britain by Clays Ltd, St Ives PLC

Headline's policy is to use papers that are natural, renewable and recyclable
products and made from wood grown in well-managed forests and other
controlled sources. The logging and manufacturing processes are expected to
conform to the environmental regulations of the country of origin.

HEADLINE PUBLISHING GROUP
An Hachette UK Company
Carmelite House
50 Victoria Embankment
London EC4Y 0DZ

www.headline.co.uk
www.hachette.co.uk

To every woman and girl who has ever been told that they cannot. You can. And you will. This book is for you.

And for two in particular who inspire me always:
Sasha and Milica.

CONTENTS

INTRODUCTION

Speaking out against inequality has never been easy. Taking action, even less so. And for women to speak out is something altogether different. History is punctuated with the scars of women's castigation, it is riven with holes where their achievements ought to be and the adversity they overcame to triumph is writ large upon its dusty pages.

Reading through most accounts of history, we could be forgiven for assuming that women were not the warriors, the great thinkers nor the pioneering scientists who shaped and changed our world. That men alone birthed art, churned out literature and fiercely challenged the status quo, while women functioned only within the domestic realm. But though the canon has perpetually erased the contribution of women and their work has been systematically discredited, devalued and derided, their light has doggedly broken through the cracks. So successfully, in fact, that the difficulty in writing this book was not in finding 100 outstanding women but in limiting their number to 100. Writing the book was an exercise in anger, sadness and frustration – but also in inspiration. I was moved to tears learning of the lengths to which women have gone for their cause, and the things that they achieved despite the odds being stacked so firmly against them.

These women who overcame seemingly insurmountable obstacles – from disability to poverty and mental ill health, from the colour of their skin to the simple fact that they were born female – by no means represent a definitive list of all those who deserve recognition. Instead, they represent an assortment of some of the most remarkable women who have left – and continue to leave – an indelible mark. In the end, the selection came down to a combination of the women's sheer achievement in their fields and a desire to represent a variety of specialisms, including those, like fashion, that are often deemed to be unimportant but in fact have an enormous impact on our culture. Each woman in this book has broken down barriers and left cracks in the glass ceiling, laying the foundations for those who followed.

Of course, everyone's favourites were an essential inclusion. Mother of the selfie and of self-expression, Frida Kahlo, never fails to inspire; creator of the modern novel and of strong impassioned female characters, Jane Austen was a no-brainer; and pop sensation Beyoncé, whose powerful anthems celebrate the sisterhood, is a modern icon. But this book was also an opportunity for these heavyweights to share their limelight with others whose contribution has long remained brushed under history's carpet – those whose Nobel Prize was usurped by their male research partner, or whose work has been eclipsed by male-dominated narratives, or whose oeuvre was long thought to be by the hand of a man. I'm talking about Lise Meitner, whose tireless resolve led to the discovery of nuclear fission; Alice Guy-Blaché, the first female film director, who developed popular cinematographic techniques; and Artemisia Gentileschi, who, when raped by her art teacher, fought back in court in an unprecedented trial, then took revenge in oil on her canvasses.

More often than not, the most overlooked are the women of colour and the underprivileged, who battled not only against the constraints of their gender to make strides but those of their race and their social standing, too. See, for example, Ida B. Wells, who was born a slave and became a famous investigative journalist, risking her life to blow the lid on lynching; underpaid Pakistani immigrant Jayaben Desai, who went on strike for two years to protest against the exploitative conditions in the factory where she worked; and one-time homeless teenager Josephine Baker, who became an international celebrity, spy and civil rights leader.

To be worthy of recognition does not require perfection. Each woman in this book is inspirational but she is not without flaws – flaws that drove her work or flaws that destroyed it. The artificial dichotomy of 'virgin or whore' only serves to hinder female progress. Instead, the acknowledgement that to be imperfect – to be human – does not diminish one's contribution is hugely important. These are renegade women who broke free from convention to achieve great things. They fought for their voices to be heard by any means available to them – whether by educating themselves when female education was forbidden, by speaking out when doing so risked incarceration, or simply by enduring public approbation for demanding equality. For this they deserve to be celebrated – flaws and all.

An extraordinary amount has changed for women over the past century. We can now own our own property, vote, stand for Parliament and take up any form of employment open to a man. What more could we possibly want? While many continue to deny the necessity of feminism today, women are still paid less than men for the same work, are expected to bear the lion's share of domestic tasks and have to fight for their reproductive rights – and that's just in the West. Elsewhere, women still endure life as second-class citizens, with one in nine girls in the developing world being married off before the age of fifteen, so-called 'honour killings' claiming the lives of over 5,000 women a year and female genital mutilation being practised in an estimated twenty-nine countries, to name a few injustices. Moreover, when women dare to speak up against such so-called 'traditions' or 'customs', they are not only lambasted but punished for doing so.

Yet it is easier than it has ever been to speak up – and it will continue to get easier still.

Today, while gender equality has still not been fully achieved and feminism remains a dirty word that some shy away from, we should look to these inspirational women who raised the spotlight on sexism and helped liberate other women – achieving just as much and often far more than their male contemporaries. The women in this book did the things that enabled us to reach this point. They were told 'no' but, nevertheless, they persisted. For this, we owe them so much.

We have heard his story, now it is time to hear *hers*. Here's to strong women. May we know them, may we be them, may we raise them – and may we always remember them.

Harriet Hall, 2017

'That brain of mine is something
more than merely mortal;
as time will show.'

ADA LOVELACE

(10 December 1815 – 27 November 1852, UK)

Mathematician and computer scientist

Although never fully recognised during her lifetime, Ada Lovelace's work prefigured modern computing and earned her the nickname the 'enchantress of numbers'.

Daughter of romantic poet Lord Byron, Lovelace was tutored in mathematics and science – subjects often forbidden for girls at the time – at the insistence of her mother. At seventeen, she met the mathematician Charles Babbage, inventor of the mechanical calculator, who was to become her mentor.

Lovelace was soon commissioned to translate a French article about Babbage's latest machine. Whilst doing so, she went one step further, supplying her own commentary on it. She theorised that Babbage's machine had the potential to translate music, pictures and text into digital form. Her notes were respected and published in 1843, but the theory within was so revolutionary that it took over a century for it to be recognised as the first computer algorithm and Lovelace as the first computer programmer.

Lovelace died, aged thirty-six, in 1852 and has since received a multitude of posthumous accolades. In 1980, the US Department of Defense named a computer language after her, and Ada Lovelace Day is celebrated every October in recognition of her groundbreaking contribution to computer technology.

'*My youth, my inexperience,
my sex, all conspired against me.*'

ALICE GUY-BLACHÉ
(1 July 1873 – 24 March 1968, France)
Film director

Though she created over a thousand films during her twenty-year career, the work of Alice Guy-Blaché remains largely unseen. Nonetheless, her contribution to cinema was fundamental.

At the age of twenty-one, while attending a screening with the Lumière brothers, Guy-Blaché became inspired to make films of her own. There and then she asked to borrow the brothers' camera and in 1894 she wrote, produced and directed her first film. *La Fée aux Choux (The Cabbage Fairy)*, a comedy about a woman who grows babies in her cabbage patch, is widely considered to be the first narrative film, making Guy-Blaché the first female director.

Throughout her career, men in the field attempted to sabotage her work but she persevered. Eventually, she moved to the United States to open her own studio, Solax, where she pioneered the use of cinematic techniques such as double exposure and fade-outs. Guy-Blaché was cited as an inspiration by Alfred Hitchcock and was awarded France's Légion d'honneur in 1953, yet following her death, her work was all but forgotten. She spent her life fighting for recognition, so when Martin Scorsese presented her with the Directors Guild of America's Lifetime Achievement Award in 2011, Guy-Blaché's contribution to cinema was finally acknowledged.

*'When you find burden in belief or
apparel, cast it off.'*

AMELIA BLOOMER

(27 May 1818 – 30 December 1894, USA)

Journalist and activist

A melia Bloomer was mercilessly mocked for wearing baggy pantaloons underneath her overskirts, but her tireless passion for dress reform planted a seed that eventually led to the acceptance of women in trousers.

After writing for her husband's progressive Quaker newspaper, Bloomer was inspired to found her own, *The Lily,* in 1849. Initially promoting temperance, the biweekly newspaper soon expanded to advocate women's suffrage and emancipation and grew so popular that its circulation quickly rose from 500 to 4,000.

In the early 1850s, a friend introduced Bloomer to the wearing of light, loose Turkish trousers under a shorter skirt. Typically consisting of layers of floor-length heavy fabric and tightly bound corsets, women's fashion of the time was cumbersome and uncomfortable. So when Bloomer saw that the knickerbockers were both modest and practical, she immediately and passionately promoted them in *The Lily.* The trousers were derogatively dubbed 'bloomers' by the press, but as cycling took off in the 1890s, more women adopted the practical style.

Bloomer remained a women's rights activist, and was credited with securing the vote for women in Ohio in 1873. Her dress reform was a pivotal step in the sartorial emancipation of women.

'Women, like men, should try to do the
impossible. And when they fail, their
failure should be a challenge to others.'

AMELIA EARHART

(24 July 1897 – disappeared 2 July 1937, USA)

Aviator

A ten-minute plane ride at a local air show in 1920 was all it took for Amelia Earhart to fall in love with flying. Afterwards, she dedicated all her efforts to saving money for flying lessons. Just six months later, Earhart bought her first plane and, the following year, climbed to 14,000 feet, breaking the world altitude record for female pilots. It was the first of many records Earhart would shatter. In 1923 she was the sixteenth woman ever to hold a pilot's licence and in 1932 became the first woman to fly solo across the Atlantic.

Earhart's achievements made her a celebrity. She dedicated herself to advancing women's aviation, becoming *Cosmopolitan*'s Aviation Editor and even designing her own clothing range. But her dream was to circumnavigate the globe so in 1937, aged thirty-nine, she set off to attempt just that. It was to be her final flight.

Earhart's plane disappeared over the South Pacific during the last leg of her journey. The plane and her body were never recovered. Conspiracy theories abound, though recent evidence suggests she landed on the island of Nikumaroro, where she made 100 calls for help until she died.

Through her dedication to aviation and to the advancement of women, Earhart inspired a generation of female pilots. Her fearless determination marks her out as a true trailblazer.

'We have no intention of stopping
this fight until we have eradicated
every single remnant of racism in
this country.'

ANGELA DAVIS

(born 26 January 1944, USA)

Writer and activist

In 1970, Angela Davis became the third woman in history to be placed on the FBI's most wanted list. She went into hiding but was found two months later by the police and incarcerated.

Davis stood accused of murder, kidnap and conspiracy connected to a courtroom shootout during the trial of George Jackson, of whose cause she was a fervent supporter. During her sixteen months in prison, worldwide demonstrations were held with the slogan 'Free Angela Davis', her plight representing that of African Americans across the country. Considered by many to have been a political prisoner, repressed for her radical civil rights activism and allegiance with the Black Panthers, Davis was soon acquitted of all charges due to a lack of tangible evidence.

It wasn't the first time Davis had experienced such prejudices. In 1969, she had been removed from her professorial role at the University of California due to her membership of the Communist Party. State governor Ronald Regan attempted to bar Davis from teaching but she fought back in court and was reinstated. In 1980 and 1984, she ran for Vice President on the Communist Party ticket.

Through her work, spanning decades, including her academia and nine books, Davis is regarded as an idol of political protest. Today, she continues to campaign for prison reform, racial equality, worker's rights and intersectional feminism.

'In spite of everything I still believe that people are really good at heart.'

ANNE FRANK

(12 June 1929 – February or March 1945, Germany)

Diarist

The girl who wrote the most poignant diary in history, Anne Frank, proved that optimism can endure through adversity. Born in Germany in 1929, Frank and her Jewish family fled to Holland in 1934 following Adolf Hitler's rise to power. In 1942, they were forced into hiding, ensconced in an annex of rooms above her father's Amsterdam office for two years. There Frank began her famous diary. She wrote about her love of beauty, of curling her hair and painting her nails. She dreamt of going outside to see the sky and of one day becoming a journalist.

On 4 August 1944, tipped off about their whereabouts, the Gestapo located the Frank family. Frank had written her final diary entry just three days prior. The family were divided and sent to concentration camps. Anne and her sister ended up in Poland's Auschwitz-Birkenau, where over 1.1 million people would eventually be slaughtered by the Nazis. The sisters were then moved to another camp, Bergen-Belsen, where they died of typhus just days apart in March 1945. Frank was fifteen years old. Just a month later, Bergen-Belsen was liberated by British troops.

After the war, Frank's diary was discovered and published. It has since been translated into sixty-seven languages, selling over thirty million copies. Her courage and *joie de vivre* in the face of unimaginable horror make it one of the most powerful memoirs ever written.

*'All women together ought to let flowers
fall upon the tomb of Aphra Behn . . . for
it was she who earned them the right to
speak their minds.'*

APHRA BEHN

(baptised 14 December 1640 – 16 April 1689, UK)

Writer

Thrown into prison in 1667, having fallen into debt working as a spy for Charles II, Aphra Behn resolved to repay her loans. To do so, she became England's first professional female writer.

In an era when women were neither writers nor breadwinners, Behn broached subjects that respectable women would not dare. She became one of the seventeenth century's most renowned playwrights, her sharp wit and prolific output making her a celebrity of the age. Behn's lyrical poetry addressed gender inequality and female sexuality, from her sheer exasperation with men to her romantic love of women.

The Disappointment (1680) tells of a man 'unable to perform' and a woman desperate to flee his advances. Her most famous work, the novel *Oroonoko* (1688), was revolutionary. Exploring slavery, race and gender, it is thought to be the first novel calling for the abolition of the slave trade, a century before it came about.

Behn continued to earn a living through writing until her death in 1689, but her work, considered scandalous, meant she was excluded from the literary canon. Largely forgotten until the twentieth century, Behn was embraced by Virginia Woolf and Vita Sackville-West as a proto-feminist, paving the way for female writers. Today, she is lauded for her fierce independence and refusal to bend to the patriarchal mould.

'As long as I live I will have
control over my being.'

ARTEMISIA GENTILESCHI

(8 July 1593 – *c.* 1656, Italy)

Artist

Artemisia Gentileschi was eighteen when she was raped by her father's friend, the artist Agostino Tassi. Gentileschi took Tassi to court in 1612, and so rare was this for the time that the seven-month trial was widely publicised. Gentileschi was physically tortured upon cross-examination and ultimately, Tassi never served his sentence but Gentileschi shines through history as a woman triumphant in a male-dominated age.

Gentileschi depicted Tassi's violent bloody murder in her paintings thereafter, transforming familiar biblical scenes into reflections of her own life such as *Judith Slaying Holofernes* (1614) in which two women mount a man, violently decapitating him. Her most famous works are those that portray female persecution, such as in *Susanna and the Elders* (1610), in which a woman is leered over by two older men. They were widely acclaimed by the Italian artistic community, and in 1616 she became the first female member of the prestigious Accademia delle Arti del Disegno in Florence. Her chiaroscuro paintings are so powerful that for centuries they were falsely attributed to her artist father, Orazio, few believing that they could have been the work of a woman's hand. Today, she is still emerging from the shadows as a feminist iconoclast for her progressive and spirited oeuvre, and is considered one of the most significant painters of the Baroque era.

'For the master's tools will never
dismantle the master's house.'

AUDRE LORDE

(18 February 1934 – 17 November 1992, USA)

Writer and activist

As a black, lesbian woman, Audre Lorde spent her lifetime fighting prejudice and promoting self-pride. Born so short-sighted as to be virtually blind, and struggling to speak, Lorde began writing first as a means of communication and later as a way to express her unique experience.

Lorde published her first volume of poetry, *The First Cities*, in 1968 to great acclaim. Two years later, her second volume explored the experiences of childbirth, motherhood and love, as well as her own sexuality – proudly coming out as gay. But it was her third volume, *From a Land Where Other People Live* (1973) that cemented her reputation as a feminist civil rights activist. The collection viscerally expressed her anger at the prejudice and oppression she had suffered as a woman of colour.

Through work that spanned poetry, critical thinking and teaching, Lorde was not afraid to point fingers at both white women and black men for being complicit in systems of oppression. In the 1980s, she founded a publishing house for women of colour and an organisation to help women under apartheid.

Lorde died in 1992, aged fifty-eight. Hers was a life hard fought and won as a social revolutionary who called for a celebration of individuality and a feminism that embraced all races and creeds.

'I will not have my life narrowed down.
I will not bow down to somebody else's
whim or to someone else's ignorance.'

BELL HOOKS

(born 25 September 1952, USA)

Writer and activist

At the age of nineteen, after a childhood spent in a segregated Kentucky neighbourhood, Gloria Watkins realised that as a young black woman she was ostracised from both the male-dominated civil rights movement and the white, middle-class-dominated feminist movement. So she penned a book about her own experiences.

She wrote under a pseudonym: bell hooks, the name of her outspoken grandmother, intentionally not capitalising the initials so that her work would focus on her theory rather than her ego. Years later, in 1981, after several rejections, *Ain't I Woman?: Black Women and Feminism* was published, and hooks' informal, accessible tone meant it quickly became a seminal text.

After completing her PhD in 1983, hooks began lecturing in African-American studies at Yale University, before teaching women's studies. In 2014, she founded the educational bell hooks institute.

During her remarkable career, hooks has published over thirty books that have radically advanced intersectional feminism, acknowledging the unique adversity faced by women of colour and underprivileged women in systems of oppression. As a result, she remains a valuable voice in the feminist movement.

'We broke through the feminine mystique and women who were wives, mothers and housewives began to find themselves as people.'

BETTY FRIEDAN

(4 February 1921 – 4 February 2006, USA)

Writer and activist

F ired for being pregnant, Betty Friedan had no choice but to put down her journalist's notebook and become a housewife. For years she stayed at home, growing increasingly dissatisfied.

Friedan wondered if her female contemporaries were experiencing similar disillusionment, so she conducted a survey of her fellow Smith College graduates. What came back was a universal feeling of frustration and dissatisfaction. Friedan had found the subject of her next article, yet every magazine turned her down. Undeterred, she used her extensive research instead as the foundation for a revolutionary manifesto, *The Feminine Mystique*. The 1963 book challenged what Friedan called 'the problem that has no name' – the curse of domesticity – and outlined the pervasive discrimination women faced. Controversial though it was, the book became a bestseller, inciting countless letters from women thanking Friedan for speaking the unspeakable. *The Feminine Mystique* sparked an international movement: second-wave feminism.

In 1966, Friedan co-founded a civil rights group, the National Organisation for Women (NOW), which aimed for reproductive rights, equal pay and improved childcare.

Friedan remained politically active until her death in 2006. At the vanguard of a movement, her invaluable work spearheaded women's liberation, changing the lives of innumerable women.

'We have to teach our girls that they can reach as high as humanly possible.'

BEYONCÉ

(born 4 September 1981, USA)

Musician

On 23 April 2016, Beyoncé dropped her sixth studio album online with no prior warning. Fearlessly broaching topics from race relations to adultery and feminism, *Lemonade* became the bestselling album of the year and racked up several awards.

Born in Texas in 1981, Beyoncé Knowles-Carter rose to fame in the mid-nineties, preaching female empowerment as one third of wildly successful R&B group Destiny's Child. Her music has reigned over the charts ever since. To date, Beyoncé has sold over 160 million records, won countless accolades and performed at numerous prestigious events, including the consecutive inaugurations of President Barack Obama.

As well as being a self-proclaimed feminist, she is outspoken in her support of gay marriage, has passionately condemned police brutality against African Americans and has opened up about the immense emotional pain of suffering miscarriage. She is a generous philanthropist, founding the Survivor Foundation to provide relief after natural disasters, and has campaigned alongside First Lady Michelle Obama.

Beyoncé is the highest-paid black musician in history and one of the most culturally relevant singers of the twenty-first century. When she speaks, the world listens. It's no wonder they call her Queen Bey.

'I am fighting as an ordinary person for my lost freedom, my bruised body, and my outraged daughters.'

BOADICEA

(died *c.* AD 61, Britain)

Warrior queen

Fearless and formidable, Boadicea rode upon her horse-drawn chariot to deliver a rallying cry for the people of Britain before what was to be her final battle.

Upon her marriage to King Prasutagus around AD 48, Boadicea had become queen of East Anglia's Iceni tribe. The occupying Roman Empire allowed Prasutagus to rule his region on the understanding that when he died, his legacy would be divided between his daughters and the Roman Emperor, Nero. However, when the day came, the Romans seized the entirety of the late Prasutagus's estate. When his widow, Boadicea, protested, she was publicly flogged and her daughters raped.

Boadicea channelled her rage into assembling a 100,000-strong army of loyal Britons, half of whom were women. She mounted an attack on the Roman stronghold of Colchester, wreaking a bloody revenge and savagely killing everyone in sight. During Boadicea's final battle in AD 61, the British army was defeated. To avoid capture, Boadicea is believed to have poisoned herself.

Though ultimately Rome prevailed, Boadicea symbolises the ultimate female warrior. Her image was used as a mascot to inspire the British suffragette movement and her valour has been preserved in a statue by Westminster Bridge, a reminder of the power of women.

'I am no bird; and no net ensnares me; I am a free human being with an independent will.'

THE BRONTË SISTERS
(Charlotte 1816 – 1855, Emily 1818 – 1848,
Anne 1820 – 1849, UK)

Writers

One dark evening in 1848, Charlotte and Anne Brontë caught the night train from Yorkshire to London. They were to meet the publishers of Currer and Acton Bell, whose novels had been widely acclaimed. What the publishers did not know was that these mystery authors were in fact the Brontë sisters.

Charlotte, Anne and Emily Brontë, together with their brother, Branwell, were raised in the West Riding of Yorkshire by their widowed father. From childhood, all four siblings composed elaborate stories for entertainment. In 1845, when Charlotte discovered a collection of Emily's poetry, she submitted them for publication with some of her and Anne's work. All three sisters adopted male aliases to disguise their gender.

Charlotte's *Jane Eyre*, with its outspoken and independent protagonist, was an immediate success upon its publication in 1847. Emily's *Wuthering Heights*, telling of a wild love affair, was published the same year and Anne's *The Tenant of Wildfell Hall* exploring an abusive marriage followed a year later.

All four siblings died prematurely, but the works of these extraordinarily talented sisters continue to fascinate, successfully capturing the mood of the Victorian era whilst depicting a timeless insight into the female condition.

'Life isn't about surviving, it's about
cramming in as much joy as possible.'

CAITLIN MORAN

(born 5 April 1975, UK)

Journalist, broadcaster, screenwriter

Home-schooled from the age of eleven, winner of the *Observer*'s Young Reporter award at fifteen, a published novelist the following year and a *Times* columnist by eighteen: Caitlin Moran's early achievements marked her out for greatness.

Growing up on a Wolverhampton council estate with her parents and seven siblings, often with little food and in the company of rats, Moran initially turned to writing as a way to entertain her brothers and sisters. At sixteen, after securing a gig as a music journalist, it became much more. A year later, Moran launched her TV career as the host of her own Channel 4 show, *Naked City*.

Perhaps her most noteworthy achievement is her 2001 book *How to Be a Woman*. An instant bestseller, the witty manifesto-cum-memoir is a no-holds-barred, rallying cry for young women that broached every topic from menstruation to masturbation and rejected feminist academic jargon. Moran became the voice of fourth-wave feminism.

Today, Moran juggles writing multiple weekly columns and screenplays and boasts numerous accolades. Dissatisfied with the dominance of the media's metropolitan elite, she speaks for the often-neglected working class. Her semi-autobiographical sitcom, *Raised By Wolves*, co-written with her sister, is a prime example of her commitment to representing the under-represented.

*'We should begin to dream about
and plan for a different world.
A fairer world.'*

CHIMAMANDA NGOZI ADICHIE

(born 15 September 1977, Nigeria)

Writer

It's rare for the words of an author to be quoted by a world-famous pop star. But when a speech by Chimamanda Ngozi Adichie was sampled in Beyoncé's song 'Flawless', it was a testament to the power of those words.

Born in Nigeria, Adichie studied medicine in her home country before devoting herself to her true passion: writing. In 2003, she published her first novel, the widely acclaimed *Purple Hibiscus*. Her second novel, *Half of a Yellow Sun* (2006), was adapted into a Hollywood film.

Yet it wasn't until 2012 that she was propelled to global fame, when she delivered her speech 'We Should All Be Feminists'. Adichie spoke about her experiences as an African woman, plainly stating the necessity of gender equality. The speech was later published as a book, and in 2016 the Swedish government distributed a copy to every sixteen-year-old child in the country. Adichie's words 'We Should All Be Feminists' were emblazoned proudly across T-shirts in Dior's Spring/Summer 2017 collection.

Adichie's unapologetic love of fashion and beauty coupled with her feminist politics prove that the two do not have to be mutually exclusive. For hers is a feminism that transcends preconceived ideas of womanhood, race and class, advocating for a celebration of all cultures and perspectives.

'Sports clothes changed our lives
because they changed our thinking
about clothes. Perhaps they, more
than anything else, made us
independent women.'

CLAIRE McCARDELL

(24 May 1905 – 22 March 1958, USA)

Fashion designer

During the Second World War, the Nazi occupation of Paris cut off the supply of French fashion to the United States. This created a demand for indigenous designers and saw the birth of the fashion style known as 'sportswear'. At the vanguard of this American movement was Claire McCardell, who developed cunning techniques in the face of fabric rationing.

McCardell offered modern women pragmatic, versatile clothing, inspired by the practicality of menswear and the comfort of sporting attire. She reappropriated fabrics from mattress ticking to denim and introduced drawstrings and brass hooks to circumvent the dearth of zippers. In a canny move, McCardell exploited dancewear's exemption from fabric rationing, incorporating leotards and ballet pumps into her designs – both now fashion staples. But her most important contribution to the history of fashion was her promotion of separates. The idea of mix-and-match wardrobes in an age of dresses allowed women to spend less but feel as though they had more, combining pieces to create a range of outfits.

McCardell's designs democratised fashion and transformed the way women dressed, putting American designers on the map. Modern designers such as Donna Karan, Calvin Klein and Stella McCartney are indebted to her philosophy.

'I will not be triumphed over.'

CLEOPATRA

(69 BC – 12 August 30 BC, Egypt)

Queen of Egypt

History paints Cleopatra as a beguiling woman who had legendary affairs with Rome's two most powerful leaders. But this telling of events overlooks her military aptitude and an intelligence that enabled her to rule a country fragmented by male-dominated political turmoil for two decades.

Coming to power at the age of eighteen, Cleopatra initially shared rule with her young brother Ptolemy XIII. The pair had conflicting views on leadership and when war broke out between them, the opportunist Julius Caesar arrived in the country with plans to extend the Roman Empire. Keen to get the upper hand, Cleopatra rolled herself inside a carpet to sneak into his chambers, then engaged her political wiles and sexual prowess to inveigle herself into his company – and his heart. The advantage was twofold: Caesar helped her overthrow Ptolemy and then he abandoned his plans of annexation.

Following Caesar's assassination, Rome was ruled by a triumvirate: Octavian, Lepidus and Mark Antony. During ensuing civil war, Cleopatra lent her support to Mark Antony, whom she later married. The pair ruled over both lands until Octavian defeated them in 31 BC. Captured, Cleopatra chose to die by exposing herself to a poisonous asp. Her death marked the passing of the only queen of the Nile and the last pharaoh of Egypt.

'A girl should be two things: who
and what she wants.'

COCO CHANEL

(19 August 1883 – 10 January 1971, France)

Fashion designer

G abrielle Chanel was taught to sew by the nuns at the orphanage where she was raised. It was a skill that set her up for life. Determined to escape her impoverished beginnings, she built a business empire from scratch and revolutionised women's fashion in the process; a literal rags-to-riches tale.

Chanel initially worked as a cabaret singer, earning her nickname 'Coco'. She romanced numerous wealthy men who helped kick-start her fashion career, and in 1910 opened her first boutique at 21 Rue Cambon, Paris. The Chanel style was unique. Her 'little black dress' reinvented the colour of mourning and she rejected the encumbering fashions of the day in favour of low-key garments that liberated the female form. Inspired by men's sporting attire, she adapted crewneck pullovers and nautical stripes for women. Her androgynous aesthetic became known as '*la garçonne*' and it dominated the 1920s.

During the Second World War, Chanel closed her couture house and holed up in the Paris Ritz with her lover, a Nazi officer. Following the war, rejected by the Parisian establishment, she fled to Switzerland. In 1953, she made a triumphant comeback. Her quilted handbag and boxy, collarless suits proved she still had the special touch and they have been reproduced the world over. Chanel reigned as the queen of couture until her death, aged eighty-seven.

'We were fighting for ourselves.'

THE DAGENHAM STRIKERS

(Active in 1968, UK)

Activists

I t started in a car factory in East London and ended in a social revolution. Rose Boland, Eileen Pullen, Vera Sime, Gwen Davis and Sheila Douglass worked together at the Dagenham Ford factory, stitching car seat covers. But a regrading scheme in 1968 stripped the women of their semi-skilled status and re-assigned them as 'unskilled' workers. This demotion came with a lower pay packet, just 85 per cent of that paid to their male counterparts. The women did not accept this discrimination.

On 7 June that year, 187 female machinists downed tools and picketed outside the factory, demanding equal pay. Despite a workforce of over 50,000, their three-week-long strike brought Ford's biggest plant in Europe to a complete standstill. The company lost over £40 million but still the bosses would not budge.

The women's resolve caught the attention of employment secretary Barbara Castle. They negotiated a pay increase from 85 to 92 per cent of male earnings and their plight inspired the steering through Parliament of the 1970 Equal Pay Act.

It was not until 1984 that the women finally achieved grading and pay equality. They had fuelled the fire of the nascent women's movement, highlighted the need for female unions, and forced the government to take notice. Today, their victory continues to inspire attempts to close the persistent gender pay gap.

'When you realise the value of all life,
you dwell less on what is past and
concentrate more on the preservation
of the future.'

DIAN FOSSEY

(16 January 1932 – *c.* 26 December 1985, USA)

Primatologist

In 1963, Dian Fossey was introduced to gorillas in the Virunga mountains by renowned palaeontologist Louis Leakey. From that moment she was determined to work with the animals. With no scientific qualifications, Fossey studied Swahili, took a crash course in primatology and joined Leakey in Rwanda. The trip turned into an eighteen-year study of gorillas and a lifetime protecting them from extinction.

Little was known about the primates, although they were thought to be highly dangerous. Fossey nonetheless immersed herself in their habitat, mimicking their behaviours in order to gain their trust, even naming them. It was not long before she was accepted. Fossey wrote about her experiences for *National Geographic*, reinventing the reputation of gorillas and providing ground-breaking insight into their human-like traits.

But others were also interested in these beautiful animals. In 1977, Fossey's favourite gorilla, Digit, was maimed by poachers. Fossey wrote about the resultant depression she suffered and spiralled into a solitary life of alcoholism. She set traps for poachers but eventually they came for her, too.

On 26 December 1985, Fossey was discovered brutally murdered in her cabin. Her killer has never been found. She now lies buried next to her beloved Digit and amongst the gorillas she helped save from extinction.

'Fashion must be the most intoxicating release from the banality of the world.'

DIANA VREELAND

(29 September 1903 – 22 August 1989, USA)

Fashion editor

Nicknamed 'ugly little monster' by her mother, Diana Vreeland capitalised on her unconventional looks with a cropped haircut and bright red lips. Vreeland had not envisaged a career in journalism but one night in 1936, decked out in Chanel, she was spotted by *Harper's Bazaar* editor Carmel Snow, who invited her to join the magazine.

After kick-starting her career with the playful column 'Why Don't You?', offering outlandish fashion and lifestyle advice, Vreeland was soon promoted to fashion editor – a post she held for twenty-five years. Never afraid to court controversy, it was she who featured the first-ever bikini in a magazine – then a shocking garment – and often referenced current affairs in her work.

In 1963, Vreeland was appointed editor-in-chief of *Vogue*, where she continued her trailblazing. She celebrated individuality over conventional beauty, discovering Twiggy and putting the then unknown Mick Jagger onto the glossy pages. In 1971, when the economy favoured a more austere outlook, Vreeland was fired. But she recovered swiftly, securing a job at the Metropolitan Museum of Art at the age of sixty-nine, where she transformed the traditional fashion exhibition. Following her death in 1989, Vreeland left behind a legacy as one of history's most revered fashion editors and a doyenne of style.

'I was captured for life by chemistry and by crystals.'

DOROTHY HODGKIN

(12 May 1910 – 29 July 1994, UK)

Chemist

T he mass production of penicillin, the treatment of diabetes and the cure of pernicious anaemia are just a few of the lifesaving medical discoveries that resulted from the pioneering work of Dorothy Hodgkin.

After falling in love with crystals during a school science class, Hodgkin went on to develop the painstaking method of protein crystallography (a process of photography that determines the structure of molecules). Hodgkin successfully used this technique to photograph insulin and penicillin. Fellow scientists refused to believe the validity of the method but her tireless resolve proved worthwhile as her pivotal discovery allowed scientists to synthetically reproduce the antibiotic and adapt it to fight many different strains of virus. In 1948, Hodgkin began investigating vitamin B12, an important step towards finding a cure for pernicious anaemia. For the subsequent breakthrough she became the first British female Nobel laureate; she was later awarded the prestigious Order of Merit.

For much of her life Hodgkin suffered from rheumatoid arthritis but, never discouraged, she continued to work from her wheelchair. In 1969, she finally determined the complex structure of insulin – around thirty-five years after she had first photographed it – a remarkable discovery that would inform the vital treatment of diabetes.

'I'll see what an ordinary English girl, without
credentials or money can accomplish.'

DOROTHY LAWRENCE

(4 October 1896 – 4 October 1964, UK)

Journalist

B inding her breasts and cropping her hair, Dorothy Lawrence climbed into uniform and transformed into Private Denis Smith. It was 1915 and Lawrence was nineteen years old.

Having been rejected as a frontline journalist on the grounds that it was too dangerous an occupation for a woman, Lawrence sought alternative means of reporting on the battlefields of the First World War. Heading to France, she befriended two soldiers who helped forge her papers, smuggle a uniform and taught her to walk like a man. As Private Smith, she joined the British Army and headed straight to the trenches. But after two weeks she fell ill and had no choice but to hand herself in. Suspected a spy, Lawrence was interrogated and sent to a convent.

Silenced until the 1918 Armistice, Lawrence published *Sapper Dorothy Lawrence: The Only English Woman Soldier* in 1919. But she continued to be unwell, suffering from post-traumatic stress disorder. When she confessed to her doctor that she'd been raped as a child, she was dismissed as a liar and committed to a mental asylum, where she spent her remaining years. Lawrence was buried in an unmarked grave in London.

Lawrence's astonishing story of determination and bravery remained relatively unknown until the centenary of the First World War but she has since been heralded as an intrepid journalist.

'Patriotism is not enough. I must have no hatred or bitterness towards anyone.'

EDITH CAVELL

(4 December 1865 – 12 October 1915, UK)

Nurse and spy

I t wasn't until a century after her death that Edith Cavell's true identity was revealed. Cavell had trained as a nurse and in 1907 was recruited to head up a new nursing school in Belgium.

At the outbreak of the First World War, Cavell was in the safe environs of Norwich visiting her father. When she heard the news, she returned immediately to Brussels to help. There she treated casualties from both sides, caring for German and Austrian soldiers without prejudice. Soon she began helping in other ways, too. Cavell and her comrades started smuggling Allied soldiers out of German-occupied Belgium, saving 200 men in a single year. In August 1915, her work was discovered by the Germans, who tried her for treason and placed her in solitary confinement. The international pressure to release Cavell was enormous, but on 12 October 1915 she confessed and was executed by firing squad. This ruthless punishment sparked outrage worldwide and she was hailed a martyr. Her death was leveraged as propaganda to drive conscription – something Cavell strongly objected to.

Upon the centenary of her death, evidence of Cavell's involvement in an espionage network was revealed. Sewn into the clothes of the soldiers she saved were secret messages that passed vital intelligence to the Allies. Today, Cavell is remembered as a war hero.

*'You can have anything you want in
life if you dress for it.'*

EDITH HEAD

(28 October 1897 – 24 October 1981, USA)

Costume designer

Responding to a job listing for a costume sketch artist, twenty-six-year-old Edith Head submitted a series of drawings to Paramount Pictures. She had no experience in costume and the illustrations were not hers. But she got the job.

Working initially on silent films, Head climbed the male-dominated ranks and in 1938 became the first woman to run the design department of a major film studio. She held the position until 1967, when she moved to Universal Pictures.

From classically elegant to outrageously ostentatious, Head's aesthetic defined the golden age of Hollywood. Dressing heavyweights including Grace Kelly and Hedy Lamarr, Head's designs were so unique that they sparked immediate trends. Alfred Hitchcock was such a fan he had her design costumes for eleven of his pictures. Her work elevated costume design to the extent that the Academy created a separate awards category for it in 1948. Head was nominated for thirty-five Oscars and won eight – more than any woman in history. Keeping the gold statuettes in her office, she called them her 'children'.

Head died in 1981 at the age of eighty-three. Her funeral was attended by Hollywood's leading lights, who bid farewell to a costume visionary and one of the most important women in cinematic history.

'Trees are not known by their leaves, nor even
their blossoms, but by their fruits.'

ELEANOR OF AQUITAINE

(1122 – 1 April 1204, France)
Queen of France and England

Not content to play the damsel in distress, Eleanor of Aquitaine, Queen of France, led an army of 300 women to Jerusalem in the Second Crusade of 1147. Despite her resolve, the crusade was a failure and it served to deepen tensions in Eleanor's marriage to Louis VII of France. Her appeal for an annulment was rejected by the Pope but in 1152, when Eleanor gave birth to a second daughter, Louis ended their fifteen-year marriage.

Soon Eleanor was betrothed to the Duke of Normandy, who became King Henry II of England. Now the Queen of England, Eleanor bore eight children and played an active role in Henry's reign. She fostered the arts, bringing poetry and music into the kingdom, reigning in the age of courtly love.

As a result of her husband's infidelities, Eleanor returned to her childhood home of Poitiers. In 1173, she led a rebellion with her son, Young Henry, to seize the throne. For this, Henry II imprisoned her for sixteen years until his death, when another of her sons, Richard the Lionheart, was crowned king. Eleanor ruled as his regent before retiring as a nun. She died aged eighty-two.

Enduring infidelity, conflict and incarceration, Eleanor of Aquitaine shrewdly exploited her connections to become the Queen of France, the Queen of England and the most powerful woman in twelfth-century Europe.

'No one can make you feel inferior
without your consent.'

ELEANOR ROOSEVELT

(11 October 1884 – 7 November 1962, USA)

Politician

E leanor Roosevelt reinvented the role of First Lady. Unwilling to sit back and perform the role of ornamental hostess to the President of the USA, she became one of the world's most celebrated humanitarians.

Born into a wealthy New York family, Roosevelt dedicated her time to philanthropy from a young age. In 1905, she married her distant cousin Franklin, and in 1933, when he entered the White House, Roosevelt took on an active role in her husband's administration. During their four terms in office – for which she became history's longest-serving First Lady – she dedicated her time to charitable causes, conducted press conferences, wrote a newspaper column and campaigned passionately for women's and civil rights. During the Second World War, she encouraged the welcoming of European refugees into the US.

Following her husband's death in 1945, Roosevelt went on to become a United Nations delegate and chair of the Human Rights Commission, helping to redraft the Universal Declaration of Human Rights. In 1961, she headed the first dedicated Presidential Commission on the Status of Women. Roosevelt authored numerous books, raised six children and remained politically active until her death, aged seventy-eight. Her work opened up new possibilities for the role of First Ladies, paving the way for the likes of Hillary Clinton and Michelle Obama.

'Men their rights, and nothing more;
women their rights, and nothing less.'

ELIZABETH CADY STANTON AND SUSAN B. ANTHONY

**(Cady Stanton 12 November 1815 – 26 October 1902,
Anthony 15 February 1820 – 13 March 1906, USA)**

Activists

Elizabeth Cady Stanton married her husband, Henry, an abolitionist, in 1840. During the ceremony, she vowed to 'love and honour' her husband but she would not 'obey', omitting this common declaration from her vows.

In 1872, Susan B. Anthony illegally cast her vote in the US presidential election. She was arrested and fined $100. But she refused to pay.

Anthony and Stanton first met at an anti-slavery convention in 1851. From then on, they campaigned tirelessly for equality, founding organisations to abolish slavery and promote women's suffrage. Stanton was the writer and Anthony the orator and organiser, travelling extensively and protesting doggedly.

Over the years they founded the American Equal Rights Association, launched weekly women's rights newspaper *The Revolution*, formed the National Woman Suffrage Association and published the multi-volume *History of Woman Suffrage*. Their activism and prolific publishing would be instrumental in driving the Nineteenth Amendment, which was ratified in 1920, finally giving women the right to vote, though sadly this was several years after their deaths. Both women are now recognised as vital catalysts to women's enfranchisement despite fierce opposition during their lifetimes.

'Punishment is not for revenge, but to lessen crime and reform the criminal.'

ELIZABETH FRY

(21 May 1780 – 12 October 1845, UK)

Prison reformer

In 1813, thirty-three-year-old Elizabeth Fry spent the night in a cold, dank cell in Newgate Prison. But she was no criminal. Fry was dedicated to improving conditions behind bars.

Fry had first visited the prison in 1812 and found hundreds of women huddled into just a few rooms, many without bedding and some with babes in arms. Shocked by the squalid conditions, Fry resolved to help the inmates, returning daily with clean clothes, teaching them skills and accompanying them to the gallows. She became known as the 'angel of prisons'.

In 1817, Fry founded the Association for the Improvement of the Female Prisoners of Newgate, which aimed to rehabilitate prisoners via education and religious study. Within a year she became the first woman to give evidence at a House of Commons committee and was granted an audience with Queen Victoria. Directly inspired by Fry's work, the 1823 Gaols Act legislated for minimum standards. Fry also lent support to the homeless and founded a nursing school that would later inspire Florence Nightingale. She died in 1845, leaving behind eleven children.

As a result of her dedication, prisons today are divided by gender, inmates undertake paid work and there is a focus on rehabilitation rather than punishment. In 2001, Fry's portrait was placed on the five pound note in recognition of her work.

'Though the sex to which I belong is considered weak you will nevertheless find me a rock that bends to no wind.'

ELIZABETH I

(7 September 1533 – 24 March 1603, England)

Queen of England

A disappointment to her father at birth due to her gender, rendered motherless at the age of two, stripped of her royal status and held prisoner in the Tower of London: Elizabeth I's path to sovereignty did not run smooth. Yet she developed into an indomitable, quick-witted woman, ascending the English throne at the age of twenty-five.

The England Elizabeth inherited was divided, bankrupt and riven with political turmoil. She faced innumerable challenges to the throne: from the Pope, from her Catholic subjects, who supported Mary Queen of Scots, and from Spanish invaders. Yet the pragmatic Elizabeth preserved peace and affluence during her forty-four-year reign. Her refusal to marry caused consternation amongst her advisors but she rejected suitor after suitor, eventually reinventing herself as an icon: the Virgin Queen.

It was during the latter years of her reign that England blossomed. She nurtured the arts and commissioned explorers to discover new trade routes; the American state of Virginia was named in her honour. Elizabeth died in 1603 at the age of sixty-nine. She named James VI of Scotland, son of Mary Queen of Scots, as her heir, thus uniting England and Scotland for the first time. Upon her death, her subjects took to the streets in mourning. England's Golden Age was over.

'I would rather be a rebel than a slave.'

EMMELINE PANKHURST

(15 July 1858 – 14 June 1928, UK)

Suffragette

B orn in Manchester in 1858 to politically engaged parents, Emmeline Pankhurst dedicated her life to the fight for women's right to vote. In 1903, following years of protests by peaceful suffragists and frustrated by the lack of progress, Pankhurst founded the Women's Social and Political Union (WSPU). This women-only organisation endorsed radical militant tactics under the motto: 'Deeds not Words'. The media condescendingly nicknamed them 'suffragettes'.

The suffragettes quickly gained notoriety for their radical activism, which included chaining themselves to railings, vandalism and arson. Pankhurst was repeatedly imprisoned as a result.

Two days after the First World War broke out, Pankhurst called a moratorium on activism, instead encouraging women to join the war effort. At the war's close, the Representation of the People Act was extended by the government to include the right to vote for property-owning women over the age of thirty as a symbol of gratitude. Later that same year, women were granted the right to be elected into Parliament.

Pankhurst died in London on 14 June 1928, aged sixty-nine, just eighteen days before women were granted equal voting rights to men. British women today owe their enfranchisement to the courage and fortitude of Pankhurst and her suffragettes.

*'I attribute my success to this – I never
gave or took any excuse.'*

FLORENCE NIGHTINGALE

(12 May 1820 – 13 August 1910, UK)

Nurse

To marry well and secure a fortune was all that was expected of women of high social standing in the 1800s. Florence Nightingale paid no heed to this patriarchal tradition. Instead, going against the wishes of her family, she enrolled as a nursing student, believing it was her divine duty to help the sick.

When the Crimean War broke out in 1853, Nightingale was called upon to organise the nursing effort. She observed the squalid conditions with horror and marshalled a complete overhaul of the system, improving supplies, sanitation and the overall quality of care. Her evening rounds, tending to patients lit by the glow of an oil lamp, earned her the nickname 'the lady with the lamp'.

On her return to England, Nightingale received a hero's welcome. But her work had only just begun. Publishing a comprehensive report on the conditions that she had witnessed, she ushered in revolutionary hospital reforms that are still practised today, before establishing a hospital and two training schools. For her altruism, she became a national icon and was awarded the Royal Red Cross and the Order of Merit. In later life, Nightingale was confined to her own sickbed, having contracted an infection in Crimea. As a result of her tireless dedication, modern British healthcare was reformed saving countless lives, and nursing was elevated from a lowly profession to the respected vocation it is today.

'There is nothing more precious than laughter. It is strength to laugh and lose oneself.'

FRIDA KAHLO

(6 July 1907 – 13 July 1954, Mexico)

Artist

At the age of six, Frida Kahlo was left with a permanent limp after contracting polio. Aged eighteen, she was riding a bus when it collided with a tram and she was impaled by a metal handrail that shattered her pelvis and fractured her spine, collarbone and ribs. For the remainder of her life – until her death at forty-seven – she suffered from chronic pain. She underwent over thirty corrective operations and spent her days bedbound wearing a back brace, but Kahlo was never deterred by the hand that life had dealt her. She refused to be a victim, channelling her suffering into bold, vibrant works on an easel suspended above her bed.

Kahlo's most famous works are her stark but colourful self-portraits, in which she wore traditional Mexican dress to celebrate her heritage. She laid bare her pain – from her multiple miscarriages to the betrayals of her husband, the celebrated artist Diego Rivera – as well as her communist ideology and intimate relationships with women. Her naïve folk style was often dubbed surrealist but Kahlo rejected the label, insisting she painted not her dreams or nightmares but her reality.

Kahlo displayed a resilience and originality that made her one of the most pivotal artists of the twentieth century. She has since become an inspiration to women and the dispossessed alike.

'You can bind my body, tie my hands, govern my actions: you are the strongest, and society adds to your power; but with my will, sir, you can do nothing.'

GEORGE SAND

(1 July 1804 – 8 June 1876, France)

Writer

A woman who dressed like a man, smoked like a man and adopted a male pseudonym, George Sand scandalised nineteenth-century French society. Born Amantine-Lucile-Aurore Dupin in 1804, Sand was raised by her mother and grandmother in the French countryside. In 1822, she married but, unsatisfied, left her husband and moved to Paris with their children. She began writing for the daily newspaper *Le Figaro*, and soon after, under the nom de plume George Sand, published her first novel, *Indiana*. It told the contentious story of a woman struggling to escape the shackles of a loveless marriage to seek true romance.

Writing prolifically and publishing her own socialist newspaper, Sand became one of the most successful female writers of the nineteenth century. Her work focused on female independence and the rebuffing of convention, reflecting her own lifestyle and recounting her passionate love affairs with various cultural figures (most notably the Polish composer Frédéric Chopin). Sand became notorious too for her sartorial style, opting for men's suits and top hats, with a cigar always in hand.

Cross-dressing, fiercely opinionated and highly regarded as a writer, George Sand defied tradition at every turn. Her radical refusal to adhere to the prescribed female role remains progressive to this day.

'A woman has two choices: either she's a
feminist or a masochist.'

GLORIA STEINEM

(born 25 March 1934, USA)

Writer and activist

D onning a satin bodice, bow tie and pert pink rabbit ears, Gloria Steinem went undercover as a Playboy Bunny. Exposing the exploitative working conditions of the faux-glamorous pin-up lifestyle, her ensuing article, 'A Bunny's Tale', was received with scorn but sparked her lifelong war on sexism.

After a poor and difficult childhood, Steinem studied politics before moving to India on a scholarship, where she developed a devotion to political activism. In 1960, she moved to New York, becoming a founding member of *New York* magazine and regularly reporting on social issues. When Steinem's column took her to an abortion hearing led by a feminist group, she became actively involved in the women's movement and was soon a leading voice of second-wave feminism.

In 1971, along with Betty Friedan, she co-founded the National Women's Political Caucus – a group advocating wage equality and reproductive freedom – and later she co-founded the hugely successful magazine *Ms.* alongside Dorothy Pitman Hughes. The radical publication became the defining magazine of 1970s feminism.

For over three decades, Steinem has championed women's liberation. On 21 January 2017, she took to the stage at the rally for the Women's March on Washington, opining that the fight for equality was not yet over.

'From then on, when anything went wrong
with a computer, we said it had bugs in it.'

GRACE HOPPER

(9 December 1906 – 1 January 1992, USA)

Computer scientist

She had tried everything to make the computer work. Peering around to examine its circuits, she found the source of the problem: a trapped moth, flapping its wings. Freeing the creature, Grace Hopper joked that she had 'debugged' the machine and the term 'computer bug' was born.

Dubbed the 'queen of code', 'the mother of computing' or simply 'Amazing Grace', Hopper was one of the first computer programmers. In 1943, with a PhD in mathematics, Hopper enlisted in the US Navy. Graduating first in her class, she was assigned lieutenant and was placed at Harvard University to work on a new computer, the Mark 1, for which she wrote the manual.

Dedicated to making computing universally accessible, Hopper's most famous contribution came a decade later in the 1950s, while she was working on the second-ever commercial computer. She created a programme that transformed computer code into a recognisable language: a compiler. It was pivotal in the development of the universal coding language used today.

Hopper died, aged eighty-five, in 1992, having received numerous accolades for her groundbreaking work, and was posthumously honoured with the Presidential Medal of Freedom. Today, as STEM subjects continue to be pegged as 'men's work', Hopper is an inspiration to women striving to topple the stereotype.

'Artists should stop making art only for the 1 per cent and start making some art for the rest of us.'

GUERRILLA GIRLS

(formed 1985, USA)

Artists and activists

I n 1985, a group of female artists stood outside New York's Museum of Modern Art. They weren't queuing for MoMA's latest blockbuster, though, they were picketing. The show, claiming to survey the history of international art, comprised just 8 per cent female artists.

Donning plastic gorilla masks and adopting the names of significant female artists, the women became the vigilante collective known as the Guerrilla Girls. Embracing activist tactics and tongue-in-cheek humour, they fly-posted New York with bold, advertisement-style posters that named and shamed galleries. Armed with statistics, the collective held talks, performances and exhibitions that highlighted the staggering under-representation of female artists. Their most famous work adapted Ingres' iconic *Grande Odalisque* (1814) to show a woman lying on a bed upon layers of opulent fabric wearing nothing but a gorilla mask, alongside the question: 'Do women have to be naked to get into the Met Museum?'

The identity of the group's members remains unknown but their striking, subversive imagery has become respected in itself, and their artistic protests have been displayed on the very walls of the institutions they criticise. After three decades of activism, the Guerrilla Girls continue to call out museums, and their radical tactics have had a lasting impact on the art world.

'There was one of two things I had a right to,
liberty, or death; if I could not have one,
I would have the other.'

HARRIET TUBMAN

(c. 1822 – 10 March 1913, USA)

Abolitionist

Harriet Tubman crossed the border into Pennsylvania with a bounty on her head, having travelled over ninety miles fleeing her slave owners in Maryland. She had no intention of returning to chains.

Born into slavery, Tubman worked as a field hand. Abused by her owners, she carried with her lifelong injuries. In 1849, Tubman made her escape to the free states in the north. But she didn't stop there. Determined to free her family and other slaves, she risked her life, returning to the south using a network of safe houses known as the Underground Railroad. Tubman made the perilous journey almost twenty times over eight years, guiding around seventy slaves to freedom and evading capture, despite the reward for her internment increasing by the day. Her courage earned her the nickname 'Moses'.

When the Civil War broke out, Tubman turned to nursing and was later recruited as a scout and a spy. After the war, she spent her meagre earnings helping former slaves and campaigned passionately for women's suffrage. An exemplar of humanitarianism and courage, Tubman's unfaltering determination and willingness to risk her own life for others earned her a place in history. In 2016 she was overwhelmingly voted to be the first African American to appear on a US banknote.

'I'm a sworn enemy of convention.'

HEDY LAMARR

(9 November 1914 – 19 January 2000, Austria)

Actor and inventor

L abelled the most beautiful woman in the world, actor Hedy Lamarr was too often underestimated. Behind the silver screen she moonlighted as an inventor, masterminding the technology that underpins Wi-Fi.

Lamarr's first marriage, to munitions tycoon Fritz Mandl, wasn't a happy one. Mandl imprisoned Lamarr in her own home while he sold weapons to the Nazis. She soon escaped to America, where she landed a lucrative contract with MGM Studios and became an overnight sensation, appearing in a series of successful films throughout the 1940s. Even so, Hollywood left Lamarr unmoved.

Keen to help with the Allied war effort, Lamarr recruited her friend George Antheil and, applying the knowledge she had eavesdropped from her ex-husband's arms deals, compiled plans for a 'secret communication system' that jumped radio frequencies to ensure missiles would be difficult to detect. In 1942, Lamarr and Antheil's invention was patented and she gifted it to the US Navy, but it lay dormant for years. The design was picked up in the 1960s and became the lynchpin of Wi-Fi, GPS and Bluetooth systems. In 1997, Lamarr and Antheil won awards for their achievements.

Lamarr died in Florida, aged eighty-six. In 2014, she was posthumously inducted to the National Inventors Hall of Fame. Without her, modern communications might be quite different.

'It is easy to be a bystander and I vowed never to be one.'

HELEN BAMBER

(1 May 1925 – 21 August 2014, UK)

Human rights activist

As a child in the 1930s, Helen Bamber was read a rather unconventional bedtime story: Adolf Hitler's *Mein Kampf*. A politically engaged Polish Jew, her father wanted her to understand the threat posed by the Nazi party.

In 1945, aged nineteen, Bamber headed to Germany's recently liberated Bergen-Belsen concentration camp to volunteer. Initially feeling powerless, Bamber soon discovered that her ability to simply listen was hugely valued by survivors, and upon her return to England she continued to counsel Holocaust victims.

In 1961, Bamber joined Amnesty International, where she set up a medical division to document the effects of state torture and lobby against governments who administered it. After three decades there, she founded the Medical Foundation for the Care of Victims of Torture, which treated upwards of 3,000 patients a year from all over the world. It was here that she pioneered a unique therapy style which helped survivors confront the horrors they'd experienced. In 1997 she was appointed an OBE.

Altruistic and resolute, Bamber formed the Helen Bamber Foundation at the age of eighty, expanding her remit to support all victims of human rights violations. After a career lasting almost seventy years, Bamber died in 2014, aged eighty-nine, leaving a mark on the world as a selfless and exceptional humanitarian.

'Until women were free of the fear of
unwanted pregnancy, they would not be able
to take up the equal opportunity of work.'

HELEN BROOK

(12 October 1907 – 3 October 1997, UK)
Family planning adviser

In 1963, Helen Brook began holding clandestine meetings with young, single women who were desperately seeking contraception. The pill had come into use in 1961, but at that time was only available to married women.

Brook volunteered at the Family Planning Association throughout the 1950s and was soon invited to head up one of the clinics. It was here that she began holding her secret meetings. When the association discovered what Brooks was up to, they insisted she find somewhere else to work. So in 1964, she set up the Brook Advisory Clinic, a safe space for women that offered contraception and sex advice to the young. The launch of the clinic caused a media scandal, with Brook accused of promoting promiscuity and adultery.

Brook was fervent in her belief that women should be liberated from the fear of unwanted pregnancy, remaining free to pursue careers should they wish. She wanted to put an end to the dangerous backstreet abortions many had been forced to seek. By 1969 her centres had helped more than 10,000 people, and she was awarded a CBE in 1995, just two years before her death. Her dedicated work broke boundaries, giving unmarried women agency over their own bodies for the first time in history.

*'The best and most beautiful things in the
world cannot be seen nor even touched,
but just felt in the heart.'*

HELEN KELLER

(27 June 1880 – 1 June 1968, USA)

Writer and activist

As cold water gushed from the pump onto Helen Keller's right hand, Anne Sullivan drew out the letters W-A-T-E-R on Keller's left hand. Using this method, deaf and blind Keller learned over thirty words by close of day.

Keller was just nineteen months old when she contracted a fever that left her without sight or hearing. Desperate to help, her parents took her to the Perkins Institute for the Blind in Boston and there they met twenty-year-old partially sighted graduate Sullivan, who became Keller's governess and lifelong companion. Sullivan penetrated the loneliness of Keller's condition, teaching her to read Braille, to sign and to speak. This teaching sparked a love of learning in Keller, who went on to become the first deaf-blind person to earn a degree in 1904, after which she published twelve books.

Keller spent her life campaigning on behalf of the disabled, as well as advocating pacifism, women's suffrage, reproductive rights and workers' rights. In 1915, she founded Helen Keller International, an organisation for the blind, and in 1920 she helped found the American Civil Liberties Union. This work earned Keller the Presidential Medal of Freedom and several honorary degrees. She died in 1968, aged eighty-seven. Despite her lack of sight, Keller was a woman whose vision changed the world.

'To all the little girls who are watching this,
never doubt that you are valuable and
powerful and deserving of every chance
and opportunity in the world to pursue
and to achieve your own dreams.'

HILLARY CLINTON

(born 26 October 1947, USA)

Politician

O n Tuesday 8 November 2016, Hillary Rodham Clinton lost the fifty-eighth American presidential election. Gracefully conceding defeat, Clinton took to the stage and told girls around the world to keep fighting to break the toughest glass ceiling.

Clinton spent her early life campaigning tirelessly for social justice and providing legal aid for the disadvantaged. When her husband, Bill Clinton, became the forty-second President of the United States in 1993, she was to be a trailblazing First Lady. She participated prominently in government work, setting up her own office in the White House to promote affordable health-care for all. In 2001, she was elected senator of New York State, the first ever US president's wife to join public office.

Clinton announced her own plans for presidency in 2007. She eventually stood down to her fellow Democratic Party member Barack Obama, but was subsequently appointed Secretary of State – a position she used to champion the education of women and girls.

Clinton ran for President once again in 2016 and became the first woman in US history to stand as the presidential nominee for a major political party. Despite securing the popular vote she did not win the presidency, but she continues to be a bastion of courage for women worldwide.

'I felt that one had better die fighting
against injustice than to die like a dog
or a rat in a trap.'

IDA B. WELLS

(16 July 1862 – 25 March 1931, USA)

Journalist and activist

In 1889, when three of Ida B. Wells's black friends were killed in jail by a lynch mob, her life found new purpose. Wells travelled across the southern USA to investigate lynching. She discovered that these death sentences were being meted out arbitrarily for even the most trivial of crimes. Horrified, she wrote about her findings and launched a campaign against those responsible. An enraged white mob attempted to intimidate Wells, but she bravely continued to speak far and wide against lynching.

Wells was born into slavery in Mississippi in 1862, just months before she and her parents were freed when slavery was abolished in 1863. Despite this, racial segregation was enforced and racism was rife. In 1884, Wells refused to concede her train seat for a white man (seventy-one years before Rosa Parks). When the conductor tried to forcibly remove her, she took him to court and won. Unfortunately, the verdict was overturned on appeal, but the incident left an indelible mark. Wells began writing, becoming one of the earliest female investigative journalists and eventually launching her own anti-racism paper, *Free Speech*, in 1889.

Ida B. Wells died in 1931 at the age of sixty-eight, having spent her life protesting injustice. Her brave activism would inspire countless others, not least those who led the African-American Civil Rights Movement of the 1960s.

'I was brought up to believe that a person must be rescued when drowning, regardless of religion and nationality.'

IRENA SENDLER

(15 February 1910 – 12 May 2008, Poland)

Wartime heroine

Disguised as a nurse, Irena Sendler smuggled Jewish children out of the Warsaw ghetto right under the Nazis' noses. In ambulances, potato sacks and even hiding a baby in a toolbox: she used every means possible to save them.

Dressed in nurse's scrubs and claiming to be treating typhoid, Sendler was able to navigate the insanitary conditions of the Jewish ghettos undetected. She saved the lives of around 2,500 Jewish children who had been destined for the death camps, giving them false names and housing them with new families. She documented their birth names, which she buried in a jar, so she could reunite them with their real families after the war.

On 20 October 1943, Sendler was arrested by the Gestapo. She was brutally tortured and sentenced to death, but managed to bribe her way to freedom and continue her clandestine work.

Despite saving more people than any other individual during the Holocaust, Sendler received little recognition until long after the war. In 2003, she was awarded Poland's Order of the White Eagle, and her bravery was acknowledged by the State of Israel. In 2008, she was also nominated for a Nobel Peace Prize. Sendler died in Poland, aged ninety-eight while tended at her bedside by a Jewish woman whom she had rescued as a baby.

*'Playing lifts you out of yourself into
a delirious place.'*

JACQUELINE DU PRÉ

(26 January 1945 – 19 October 1987, UK)

Cellist

Jacqueline du Pré stopped playing the cello at the age of twenty-eight, at the height of her fame. Her career lasted less than a decade but she had already become one of the most celebrated classical musicians of the twentieth century.

Having heard a cello performance on the radio, four-year-old du Pré asked her mother for one. The following year she started lessons and at eleven she won her first competition. It was her 1962 Royal Festival Hall performance of Elgar's Cello Concerto that defined her career. Playing with passionate confidence, precision and ferocity, du Pré's rendition of the concerto eclipsed earlier versions. A meteoric rise to fame followed, as she performed with the most esteemed orchestras across the world. When she married conductor and pianist Daniel Barenboim in 1967, the pair became the golden celebrity couple of the 1960s.

The glory years came to an abrupt end in 1971, when loss of sensitivity in her hands forced du Pré to take a sabbatical. She was diagnosed with multiple sclerosis. Miserable, du Pré turned to teaching and aiding MS research. Within years she was virtually paralysed, unable to speak and requiring twenty-four-hour care. After a fifteen-year struggle, du Pré died to the sound of music, aged forty-two. Her electrifying performances live on and inspire classical musicians to this day.

'There is a stubbornness about me that
never can bear to be frightened at the
will of others. My courage always rises
at every attempt to intimidate me.'

JANE AUSTEN

(6 December 1775 – 18 July 1817, UK)

Writer

'It is a truth universally acknowledged that a single man in posses-sion of a good fortune must be in want of a wife.' The opening words of Jane Austen's grandest achievement might have fallen into cliché, but this stands as testament to their enduring popularity.

From early childhood, Austen would scribble stories mocking the customs and conventions of Georgian society and recite them to entertain her seven siblings. By twenty she had com-pleted first drafts of two novels. In 1797, her father submitted *Pride and Prejudice* for publication but it was rejected. It was not until fourteen years later that Austen's first work, *Sense and Sensibility*, was published anonymously, as was the custom for canny female authors of the era.

Austen's shrewd observation and sharp satire magnified the mundane. Filled with complex female characters, her works critiqued the subordinate position of women in society and showcased new literary techniques. But her novels received mixed reviews and sold moderately.

Austen died in 1817, aged forty-one. Her brother disclosed her identity but Austen's work saw scant recognition. The true extent of her insight would not be appreciated until the twen-tieth century. Today, she is considered one of the greatest novelists in the English language.

'We are those lions, Mr Manager.'

JAYABEN DESAI

(2 April 1933 – 23 December 2010, India)

Activist

The stagnant air lay thick with dry heat on the factory floor. The summer of 1976 was one of the hottest on record in Britain, and Jayaben Desai had been working all day in a room without air-conditioning. When her supervisor demanded she do overtime, it was the final straw.

Walking out of the Grunwick Film Processing Laboratories in Willesden, London, Desai rallied her colleagues to leave with her. The following morning they set up a picket line outside the factory.

The Grunwick walkout was the catalyst that sparked a two-year protest by South Asian female workers, who became known as the 'strikers in saris'. They protested against unfair sackings, poor pay and unlawful working conditions. These determined women eventually gained the support of the unions, politicians and even the Post Office, which boycotted Grunwick. At the strike's peak, 20,000 people marched in support of their plight.

While Desai and her colleagues didn't succeed in their particular battle, they won another. Desai had taken on the establishment, standing up against exploitation and institutionalised racism. She spearheaded a movement that had a lasting impact on the treatment of migrant workers in the UK and shattered the stereotype of the subservient Indian woman.

'It is impossible to live without failing at
something, unless you live so cautiously that
you might as well not have lived at all – in
which case, you fail by default.'

J. K. ROWLING

(born 31 July 1965, UK)

Writer

It was whilst sitting on a delayed train from Manchester to London in 1990 that Jo Rowling dreamed up the literary phenomenon of a century. She could see a boy with a mop of dark hair and a lightning-bolt scar in her mind's eye but, without a pen, Rowling had to wait until she got home before she could first write down the name of the boy who lived: Harry Potter.

Following a divorce, Rowling moved to Edinburgh, a single parent surviving on welfare. It was under these unassuming circumstances that she brought her wizarding world to life, writing daily in a cafe whilst her baby daughter slept beside her. Rowling submitted her manuscript for *Harry Potter and the Philosopher's Stone* to numerous agents, but the rejections rolled in. Determined, she persevered and in 1996 a publisher agreed to a small print run, abbreviating her name to initials so as to belie her gender. J. K. Rowling was born.

By 1999 Rowling had become the first author in history to occupy the top three slots in the *New York Times* bestseller list, and Warner Brothers had bid for the film rights. The following year, the fourth Harry Potter instalment became the fastest-selling book in history. Today, she boasts an OBE and a roster of honorary degrees. From an idea hatched on a delayed train to a publishing phenomenon. That's quite some journey.

'It was for this that I was born!'

JOAN OF ARC

(*c.* 1412 – 30 May 1431, France)

Warrior and saint

On 30 May 1431, a crowd of 10,000 people stood in the marketplace in Rouen, France, and watched as flames licked over the body of nineteen-year-old Joan of Arc.

Born a peasant in 1412, during the Hundred Years War between France and England, Joan of Arc was beset by visions encouraging her to lead a devout life. At the age of thirteen, Joan believed she had been visited by saints with a message from God that she was the chosen saviour of France. She persuaded the French heir, Dauphin Charles, that she could expel the English from their country and bring him to the throne. In 1429, aged seventeen, wearing men's armour and with freshly cropped hair (and no military training), Joan led French troops to victory in battle against the English at the besieged city of Orléans. After several battles, Charles VII was crowned King of France.

In 1430 Joan was taken captive and sold to the English, who imprisoned her. She was charged with witchcraft, heresy and with dressing like a man. The sentence was death by pyre.

The Hundred Years War continued long after Joan's death and she was eventually exonerated of her crimes and proclaimed a martyr. In 1920, some 500 years after her death, Joan of Arc was canonised by the Pope, becoming the patron saint of France.

'It was a tribute to her ability that her equality with the men was never in question, even in those unenlightened days.'

JOAN CLARKE

(24 June 1917 – 4 September 1996, UK)

Cryptanalyst

The work of Joan Clarke is relatively unknown, but she played a vital role in breaking the code that eventually led to the end of the Second World War.

Despite receiving a double first in mathematics at Cambridge University, Clarke was not awarded a fully-fledged degree – that honour being reserved only for men at the time. Nonetheless, her brilliant mathematical mind resulted in her recruitment to the top-secret Government Code and Cypher School at Bletchley Park. The sole purpose of the GCCS was to break the German Enigma Code.

The code was believed to be unbreakable. The Enigma machine sent messages that directed German U-boats to sink Allied ships and it reset every twenty-four hours. The longer it took to crack the code, the more lives were lost. Clarke joined the Hut 8 team (led by Alan Turing) as one of very few female cryptanalysts and by 1944 was appointed deputy head. The pressure was immense but the crucial work of Clarke and her colleagues meant the Allies were able to decode messages before Hitler even saw them, saving countless lives and shortening the war.

Following the war, Clarke worked at the Government Communications Headquarters and was appointed a Member of the British Empire in 1947. The 2014 film *The Imitation Game* posthumously honoured her vital role at Bletchley Park.

*'I did take the blows [of life], but I took them
with my chin up, in dignity, because I so
profoundly love and respect humanity.'*

JOSEPHINE BAKER

(3 June 1906 – 12 April 1975, USA)

Performer, spy, activist

C limbing down from a palm tree onto the stage, Josephine Baker delighted the audience of Paris's Folies Bergère with her performance. Wearing a skirt made from sixteen bananas, she presented the stereotyped image of an African-American woman. Using her otherness to her advantage she became an overnight sensation, nicknamed 'Black Pearl'.

From an impoverished childhood in St Louis, Baker moved to her adoptive home of France, where she danced, sang, acted and walked the streets with her pet cheetah in tow. During the Second World War, her celebrity enabled her to spy for the French Resistance and smuggle intelligence written in invisible ink on her sheet music – work that earned her the Légion d'honneur.

Returning to the US, Baker was horrified by segregation and dedicated her time to the fight for civil rights, speaking alongside Martin Luther King Jr at rallies. Following his assassination, she was asked to lead the movement but declined, fearing for her children's safety.

Baker dreamed of a world of racial harmony. She adopted a cadre of twelve children of different ethnicities, calling them her 'Rainbow Tribe', and they lived in a château in the south of France. On her death in 1975, over 20,000 people took to the streets of Paris to watch her funeral procession.

'If you obey all the rules, you miss all the fun.'

KATHARINE HEPBURN

(12 May 1907 – 29 June 2003, USA)

Actor

Katharine Hepburn broke all the rules, rejecting the stereotype of the glamorous film star to create an entirely new female role model. After a rocky start to her career that saw her fired from her first stage play, Hepburn soon attracted the attention of Hollywood and was signed up to play a raft of strong female characters. She won her first Academy Award in 1934, at just twenty-six.

Hepburn was an elusive, outspoken woman who refused to work for less than $1,000 a week, preferred to go without make-up and performed her own stunts. While off screen, she avoided the limelight and famously spent most of her time dressed in trouser suits – a highly subversive move for a woman in the 1930s.

While fashion magazines lauded her style, Hepburn's slacks had her labelled 'box office poison', and she found herself losing roles. Undeterred, she returned to the stage in *The Philadelphia Story*, a play so widely acclaimed that she bought the film rights and made a triumphant return to Hollywood in 1940 with another Oscar nomination.

Hepburn scored an incredible twelve Oscar nominations in her career, and four wins – the record for a female actor. She acted in her final role in 1994 and died at the age of ninety-six.

'I counted everything: the steps, the dishes, the stars in the sky.'

KATHERINE G. JOHNSON

(born 26 August 1918, USA)

Physicist and mathematician

K atherine Johnson was the only person astronaut John Glenn would listen to before boarding the Mercury *Friendship 7* and heading into space. A computer had calculated his ship's trajectory, but he wanted a second opinion. 'Get the girl,' he said.

Johnson checked the numbers and gave the go-ahead. The mission was a success and in 1962 Glenn became the first person to orbit the Earth. The preceding year, Johnson had plotted the flight path of America's first manned space mission.

Growing up in West Virginia, Johnson's educational opportunities were restricted by her race, but she was a gifted student and finished school four years early, later being handpicked as one of three black students to attend a white-only university. At NASA, Johnson's complex calculations were vital to the success of the historic moon landing of 1969. When the Apollo 13 malfunctioned, her by-hand sums determined its safe return. But still she faced racial prejudice at work.

In 2015, almost thirty years after she'd retired, Johnson was awarded the Presidential Medal of Freedom. The following year, NASA named a new research facility after her. Her legacy truly came to light in the 2016 Oscar-nominated film *Hidden Figures*, which brought her story of triumph over racial segregation to the masses and cemented her well-deserved place in history.

'This is not a story of misery. This is a story
of how strong the human mind can be.'

KATIE PIPER

(12 October 1983, UK)

Philanthropist

In 2009, Katie Piper waived her right to anonymity and decided to tell her story. The resulting Channel 4 documentary, *Katie: My Beautiful Face,* told of the horrific attack she had experienced when she was just twenty-four.

Whilst walking in the street, a stranger had thrown a cup of industrial-strength sulphuric acid in Piper's face. The act had been orchestrated by a man she had met just two weeks earlier. Piper had been an aspiring model and television presenter, but the sickening attack left her blind in one eye, with third-degree burns and a closed oesophagus. She was rushed to hospital and put into a medically induced coma for twelve days. When she woke up, she handed her mother a piece of paper that simply said: 'Kill me'.

Following hundreds of operations and months wearing a plastic mask, Piper refused to be a victim. Instead, her recovery marked the beginning of a new life of philanthropy, dedicated to helping burns victims and tearing down beauty standards.

Since then, Piper has authored several books detailing her ordeal and her struggle to overcome it, presented television programmes and launched her own charity, the Katie Piper Foundation, which helps people living with burns and scars. Her attacker and his accomplice are serving life sentences. Piper is a survivor and her courage and resilience prove beauty is only skin deep.

*'If your compliments are making women
feel uncomfortable, scared, anxious,
annoyed or harassed, you're probably
not doing them right.'*

LAURA BATES

(born 27 August 1986, UK)

Writer and activist

I n 2012, fed up with people telling her that women were now equal in society, Laura Bates appealed to women to send her their stories of the casual sexism they had encountered in order to reveal its pervasiveness. Bates had expected just a handful of replies but what she got was a deluge.

Bates quickly became a figurehead of modern feminism, speaking widely, lobbying and writing prolifically. Her work sparked tangible change. With the extent of abuse on public transport exposed, London added a further 2,000 transport officers to buses and trains, which led to a 20 per cent increase in the reporting of occurrences. Bates also successfully campaigned for compulsory sex education in schools to stamp out sexism and issues surrounding consent from a young age. Today, the Everyday Sexism Project has hundreds of thousands of Twitter followers, a blog and factions in over twenty-five countries and the term 'everyday sexism' has entered the modern vernacular.

In 2014, Bates published the *Everyday Sexism* book, which was followed in 2016 by *Girl Up*, a feminist manual for young women that soared straight to the top of the bestseller list. In 2015, she was awarded the British Empire Medal for her work. Despite the abuse Bates receives on a daily basis from online misogynists, she continues to fight, undeterred, for that very simple concept: gender equality.

'Naturally I took pictures. What's a
girl supposed to do when a battle
lands in her lap?'

LEE MILLER

(23 April 1907 – 21 July 1977, USA)

Photographer

Taking off her combat boots, thick with the mud of the liberated Dachau concentration camp, Lee Miller strips down and climbs into Adolf Hitler's bathtub to rinse off . . . and pose for a photograph. The resulting image is a defiant middle finger to the Führer, and a snapshot of a bohemian trailblazer.

At the age of nineteen, whilst at art school, Miller was discovered by Condé Nast himself, who requested she pose for American *Vogue*. After a brief career as a sought-after fashion model, she grew tired of life in front of the lens. She moved to Paris, where she apprenticed for the surrealist frontrunner Man Ray, later becoming his lover and muse. Miller also famously had affairs with Charlie Chaplin and Pablo Picasso, and she appeared in one of Jean Cocteau's surrealist films.

At the outbreak of the Second World War, Miller became the official war correspondent for *Vogue*, documenting the conflict and women's role within it. Accompanying the Allied forces into Germany in 1945, Miller captured the atrocities of the concentration camps in harrowing images that would take a heavy toll on her mental state.

Miller's later life was largely defined by depression and alcoholism, but she never spoke about her experiences. She is remembered as one of the most acclaimed photographers of the twentieth century.

'There is no such thing as a perfect feminist, and I am no exception.'

LENA DUNHAM

(born 13 May 1986, USA)

Actor, writer, director

In 2012, the hit show *Girls* revolutionised the way women were portrayed on the small screen. Written, produced, directed by and starring Lena Dunham, it depicted the lives of four women navigating the labyrinth of twenty-something existence. *Girls* wasn't afraid to present an unapologetic, startlingly honest image of womanhood. Sex was awkward, jobs were dead-end and oblivious privilege was omnipresent. It was *Sex and the City* for millennials and Lena Dunham took home two Golden Globes for it.

Dunham started writing and making short films from a young age. At twenty-three, she created her first feature-length film, *Tiny Furniture* but *Girls* catapulted her to global fame. By 2012 she had signed a multi-million-pound book deal for her confessional memoirs, *Not That Kind of Girl*, broaching topics from sexual consent to body positivity. In 2015, she launched her own production company, podcast and newsletter, *Lenny Letter*, commissioning celebrities and politicians to contribute.

Alongside her professional success, Dunham campaigned for Hillary Clinton's presidential bid, tirelessly advocates reproductive autonomy and is known for her unflinchingly frank social media accounts that detail her struggle with mental health. Her self-abasement has made her a real-life anti-heroine and feminist figurehead; the voice of her generation.

*'I love physics with all my heart . . . It is a kind
of personal love, as one has for a person to
whom one is grateful for many things.'*

LISE MEITNER

(7 November 1878 – 27 October 1968, Austria)

Nuclear physicist

In 1901, Austria lifted its ban on female university applicants. Lise Meitner was among the first to matriculate. By 1905, aged twenty-seven, Meitner had obtained her PhD, becoming one of just a handful of women in the world to have one.

Two years later, she moved to Berlin and met the chemist Otto Hahn, with whom she would partner for the next thirty years. In 1917, they discovered the element protactinium and later that year the pair began pioneering work in radioactivity. But the Nazi annexation of Austria forced Meitner – a Jew – to flee to Sweden. From there she continued to work secretly with Hahn, determined to divide uranium into different elements. In 1939, the pair split the atom for the first time in history and coined the term 'nuclear fission' – a process still used to create energy today. Devastatingly, their discovery provided the means to develop nuclear warfare. Meitner was horrified at being dubbed 'the mother of the atomic bomb' and condemned this use of her own research.

When Hahn published their findings, he did so without citing Meitner as co-author and in 1944 he alone was awarded the Nobel Prize. Although Meitner received many accolades in her lifetime, the Nobel Prize that should have been hers casts a shadow over the memory of a brilliant scientist.

*'They thought that the bullets would
silence us, but they failed.'*

MALALA YOUSAFZAI

(born 12 July 1997, Pakistan)

Activist

On 9 October 2012, a masked gunman boarded the school bus that fifteen-year-old Malala Yousafzai was riding and shot her point-blank in the head, leaving her for dead.

The Taliban had taken her hometown – in Pakistan's once-idyllic Swat Valley – under their reign of terror in 2007, denying young women an education and destroying 400 institutions. In 2009, eleven-year-old Malala began speaking publically in support of education and blogging for BBC Urdu about the horrors of life under Taliban rule, adopting the pseudonym Gul Makai. Later the same year she revealed her true identity and campaigned openly for girls' education. At fourteen, she was awarded Pakistan's National Youth Peace Prize. As a consequence of her activism, the Taliban issued multiple death threats against her.

Miraculously, Malala survived the shooting. Undeterred, she travelled the world lobbying global leaders to promote her cause. Her efforts resulted in the first Right to Education Bill in Pakistan. Malala's book *I am Malala* became an international bestseller in 2013 and a year later, aged just seventeen, she became the youngest-ever recipient of the Nobel Peace Prize. Today, despite persistent threats from extremists worldwide, the girl who was shot for going to school continues to fight for female education.

'They just messed with the wrong woman.'

MANAL AL-SHARIF

(born 25 April 1979, Saudi Arabia)

Activist

M anal al-Sharif takes off the handbrake, puts the car into first gear, pulls out into the street and drives around her home city of Khobar. For this simple act, she could be arrested.

It's 2011 and in Saudi Arabia women are forbidden to drive. Al-Sharif doesn't hide, though. Instead, she has her friend Wajeha al-Huwaider film her while she rails against the misogynistic Saudi government, urging other women to do the same. She then uploads the video to the Internet.

Al-Sharif's video received millions of views. Her Facebook group organised a 'Women2Drive' campaign for 17 June 2011 that quickly racked up 12,000 fans. Al-Sharif was arrested and jailed for nine days, released on the condition she would not drive again. But by then her message had spread. On 17 June, 100 Saudi women bravely got behind the wheel in defiance of the ban and posted pictures and videos of themselves driving. In November 2011, al-Sharif filed the first lawsuit against the Saudi Directorate of Traffic for not permitting her a driving licence. Fired from her job and receiving daily threats, al-Sharif refused to be deterred. Her feminist pressure group, My Right to Dignity, calls for the end of decades-long Saudi male guardianship and challenges Islamic extremism.

In 2017, King Salman of Saudia Arabia lifted the driving ban. Al-Sharif posted a celebratory picture of herself behind the wheel.

'*There was no choice but to be pioneers.*'

MARGARET HAMILTON

(born 17 August 1936, USA)

Computer scientist

Alarms pierced through the spacecraft warning of imminent disaster. Outside the vessel the cold, airless Milky Way lay in wait. The astronauts on board the Apollo 11 knew that this might be the end.

But Margaret Hamilton – systems engineer and leader of the team that created the onboard flight software – had anticipated this moment. Her software kicked into gear. Three minutes later, the alarms stopped and, on 20 July 1969, Neil Armstrong and Buzz Aldrin made history as the first people to set foot on the moon.

Hamilton initially worked in software as a means to support her family, often bringing her four-year-old daughter to the lab. Programming was then considered a feminine pursuit, so Hamilton coined the term 'software engineering' to lend her job gravitas. She and her 100-strong team would go on to handwrite the world's first portable computer code. Her system was so robust that it was used for all Apollo missions and was adapted for aeroplanes.

It wasn't until 2003 that Hamilton was finally acknowledged for developing the fundamentals of software engineering, receiving NASA's Exceptional Space Act Award. In 2016, President Barack Obama presented her, aged eighty, with the Presidential Medal of Freedom. One giant leap for women in tech.

'Nothing in life is to be feared; it is only
to be understood.'

MARIE CURIE

(7 November 1867 – 4 July 1934, Poland)

Physicist and chemist

The first woman in history to win a Nobel Prize and the first person to win two, Marie Curie worked on pioneering research that resulted in life-saving cancer treatments.

Born in Warsaw, Poland, Curie had a thirst for knowledge that led her to study physics and mathematics at Paris's Sorbonne. There she met fellow scientist and her future husband Pierre Curie, who gave up his own experiments to focus on Curie's investigations into radioactivity (a word she invented). Together they discovered two new chemical elements: polonium and radium, and in 1903 the couple was awarded the Nobel Prize in Physics. In 1906, Pierre died in a road accident and Curie took over his job as a professor, becoming the first woman to teach at the Sorbonne. In 1911, she received a second Nobel Prize, this time in Chemistry.

During the First World War, Curie developed X-ray machines that were taken to the frontlines and she became head of the Red Cross radiological service. She later grew unwell as a result of radiation exposure and died in France, aged sixty-six. She was the first woman to be buried in the Panthéon in Paris.

Curie spent much of her life battling male opposition, never truly reaping financial rewards for her work. Despite this, her work revolutionised the face of modern medicine, and today the Marie Curie Foundation strives to cure cancer in her name.

'*To me, the only sin is mediocrity.*'

MARTHA GRAHAM

(11 May 1894 – 1 April 1991, USA)

Dancer and choreographer

It was only at the age of twenty-two, following the death of her disapproving father, that Martha Graham was able to pursue her dream of becoming a dancer. She went on to dance for over fifty years, choreographing over 180 ballets and earning the moniker 'the mother of modern dance'.

At a time when ballet typified women as doll-like ornaments, Graham created something radically new: dance that expressed sensuality and raw emotion. Her dynamic, jarring style – today considered revolutionary – was initially regarded as obscene and ugly. Drawing inspiration from a diverse range of cultures, her movement reflected the core of the human condition. She explored Greek mythology and Freudian theory, her female characters drove the narrative and her males were merely subordinate.

Graham was non-traditional in every sense of the word. She created the first multicultural dance school, boycotted the 1936 Berlin Olympics in protest against Hitler, exchanged the decorative ballet tutu for dramatic dark clothing, and shunned painful ballet pointes for bare feet. Dancing until well into her seventies and choreographing until her death, aged ninety-six, Graham won numerous awards for her work and was awarded the Presidential Medal of Freedom in 1976. Today, the Graham technique is one of the most widely taught styles of contemporary dance.

'The carpenter's daughter has won a name
for herself, and has deserved to win it.'

MARY ANNING

(21 May 1799 – 9 March 1847, UK)

Palaeontologist

Jutting out from a block of shale on the beach at Lyme Regis, the menacing skull of a crocodile-like creature looked up at twelve-year old Mary Anning. She had happened upon the beast whilst walking with her brother in 1811. Over the course of several months Anning returned to the beach, gently chipping away at the rock until, eventually, an entire skeleton was revealed. This creature did not have legs, like a crocodile, but the fins and tail of a fish. What young Anning had discovered was the first complete example of a fossilised ichthyosaur, or fish-lizard.

Too poor for a formal education, Anning was an autodidact. Each time she found a new fossil, she would analyse it and draw it. She sold her specimens to palaeontologists and soon experts began to visit her, seeking her opinion. Anning was dubbed the 'princess of palaeontology'. Despite the crucial role she played in the field, Anning was not eligible to join the male-only Geological Society of London, her contributions were cast aside and she remained poor. When her legacy was posthumously rediscovered, her story inspired the children's tongue-twister 'She sells seashells on the seashore'.

Anning died in 1847, aged forty-seven. Today, she is recognised as one of the foremost contributors to British science, whose findings would eventually lead to our understanding of evolution.

*'Fashion is not frivolous. It is a part
of being alive today.'*

MARY QUANT

(born 11 February 1934, UK)

Fashion designer

A miniskirt might not seem like much of a rebellion, but in the 1960s it was outrageous and Mary Quant had every fashion-conscious woman in London wearing one, defining the Swinging Sixties style.

Quant opened her boutique, Bazaar, on the King's Road in 1955 at the age of twenty-one. Here she sold quirky, colourful, affordable clothes in a bid to democratise fashion. It was the miniskirt that defined Quant and it became the symbol of sexual liberation. It shocked older generations – including Chanel, who dismissed it as vulgar – but it took the fashion world by storm. Quant was undetered, soon after creating hotpants.

Her bright geometric prints, coquettish dresses with Peter Pan collars and knee-high patent boots became known as the 'Chelsea Look'. In 1963, Quant was approached by a US department store and her clothes were sold worldwide, creating a multi-million-pound business, for which she was awarded an OBE in 1966.

Quant instilled a new awareness in fashion – the importance of the youth market – and was at the vanguard of a seismic shift in fashion history known as the Youthquake. It was largely thanks to Quant that fashion was no longer dictated from the top down, and her designs injected some much-needed frivolity into fashion.

'The grateful words and smile which rewarded me for binding up a wound or giving a cooling drink was a pleasure worth risking life for at any time.'

MARY SEACOLE

(1805 – 14 May 1881, Jamaica)

Nurse

M ary Seacole packed a bag and headed to the battlefield. She had heard about the devastating number of soldiers dying from cholera in Crimea and was determined to help. Seacole arrived at the frontline in 1854 and founded the British Hotel, selling provisions, offering shelter and tending to the wounded, earning the nickname 'Mother Seacole'.

Born in Kingston, Jamaica, in 1805, as a child Seacole worked alongside her mother in a boarding house where they provided medical care for wounded soldiers, later travelling to help the sick.

After the Crimean War ended, Seacole returned to England, bankrupt. Her story was publicised in a newspaper article in 1856, sparking a groundswell of support from the military, which resulted in a four-day benefit in her honour. Soon after, she published her memoirs, *Wonderful Adventures of Mrs Seacole in Many Lands*, the first autobiography written by a black woman in Britain. It was a bestseller.

Seacole died in London in 1881 and her legacy fell into obscurity, overshadowed by the work of Florence Nightingale. In 1991, she was posthumously awarded the Jamaican Order of Merit. She was voted the greatest black Briton in 2004, and in 2017 a statue of her was erected in London, celebrating the achievements of this selfless woman.

'Age has not abated my zeal for the emancipation of my sex from the unreasonable prejudice too prevalent in Great Britain against a literary and scientific education for women.'

MARY SOMERVILLE

(26 December 1780 – 29 November 1872, UK)

Mathematician and astronomer

K nown as the 'queen of nineteenth-century science', Mary Somerville paved the way for the advancement of women in science and the common understanding of many complex theories. Raised in an age when women were rarely educated, Somerville was virtually illiterate until, flicking through a women's magazine at fifteen, she discovered algebra. Much to the chagrin of her father, she began her own studies. In 1807, inheritance from the death of her husband went towards her passion for mathematics and astronomy.

Nineteen years later, married to her supportive second husband, William Somerville, she published her first scientific paper. William presented it to the Royal Society on her behalf, as women were forbidden to do so. Somerville's *On the Connection of the Physical Sciences* (1834) was to have a lasting impact on astronomy. The polymath noticed that the orbit of Uranus suggested another planet must be in the vicinity, inspiring the scientist who ultimately discovered Neptune. Her 1848 book, *Physical Geography*, was the first English-language geographical book and was used in schools for over fifty years.

Somerville died in 1872, at the age of ninety-one. In 1879, Oxford University named the first women's college after her, and in 2016 she was voted to become the first non-royal woman on the Scottish £10 note.

'I do not wish [women] to have power
over men; but over themselves.'

MARY WOLLSTONECRAFT

(27 April 1759 – 10 September 1797, UK)

Writer

Raised by a drunk and abusive father who squandered the family's money and denied her a proper education, Mary Wollstonecraft resolved to learn and to earn her own livelihood. After pursuing a range of careers, Wollstonecraft eventually settled upon writing, publishing her first book, the didactic *Thoughts on the Education of Daughters,* in 1787.

It was her 1792 work, *A Vindication of the Rights of Woman*, which brought her fame. Positing women's political, social and economic emancipation, it sparked great controversy. During a time when women were denied autonomy, it was a bold move to challenge traditional patriarchal structures and the subservient role of women and to advocate educational reform. Wollstonecraft was ridiculed by many and her later book, *Maria, or the Wrongs of Woman,* a radical novel that conceived that women had the same powerful sexual desires as men, was received with alarm.

Wollstonecraft's personal life – in which she twice attempted suicide and had two illegitimate children (including Mary Shelley, who would go on to author *Frankenstein*) – was used by dissenters in attempts to discredit her work. It wasn't until over a century after her death that her writing was fully appreciated. Today, *A Vindication* is widely considered the first British feminist text and Wollstonecraft, the mother of feminism.

'Matilda tested the presupposition of male sovereignty, almost to destruction.'

THE EMPRESS MATILDA

(*c.* 7 February 1102 – 10 September 1167, England)

Empress

Granddaughter of William the Conqueror, Matilda was following in her grandfather's footsteps when in 1139 she invaded England to claim her right to the throne. The dispute resulted in nineteen years of civil war, known as The Anarchy.

Matilda had assumed the title of Empress when her father, Henry I, married her off as a child to the Holy Roman Emperor Henry V. In 1120, disaster struck the English monarchy when Matilda's twin brother drowned on the *White Ship*, resulting in a succession crisis. Matilda remained Henry's only legitimate heir, but on Henry's death in 1135 Matilda's cousin Stephen seized the throne with support from the Church.

Determined to assume her rightful place as the first Queen of England, Matilda crossed from France with an army. England was thrown into civil war. Matilda fought for her birth right until 1148, when she returned to Normandy, leaving her son Henry to press on. In 1153, a truce was brokered whereby Stephen remained king but recognised Matilda's son as his successor. A year later, the latter was crowned Henry II. Matilda remained his unofficial regent and advisor until her death in Rouen in 1167.

It wasn't until 400 years later in 1553 that England's first official queen – Mary I – was crowned, but the legacy of Matilda's resourcefulness and determination lives on.

'Human beings should understand how
other humans feel no matter where they are,
no matter what their language or culture is,
no matter their age, and no matter the age
in which they live.'

MAYA ANGELOU

(4 April 1928 – 28 May 2014, USA)

Writer and activist

O n 20 January 1993, Maya Angelou took to the podium in Washington, DC, at the inauguration of President Bill Clinton and delivered her poem 'On the Pulse of Morning'. It called upon the new administration to honour diversity and equality, cementing her as an international force.

Angelou was already a renowned writer, having received acclaim for 1969's *I Know Why the Caged Bird Sings*, the first of six autobiographical works that chronicled her childhood and described the troubled race relations in the southern states.

Throughout her life, Angelou wrote poignant poems that celebrated the strength of women and addressed civil rights issues. Her spoken performances earned her several Grammy awards. She also wrote, produced and performed in productions for the theatre, film and TV. In 1972, she became Hollywood's first black female director.

Angelou dedicated much of her life to the fight for civil rights, working closely with Malcolm X and Martin Luther King Jr and serving on two presidential committees. Her myriad accomplishments brought numerous awards, including Emmy, Tony and Pulitzer Prize nominations. She was the recipient of over fifty honorary degrees and in 2010, four years before her death, she was awarded the Presidential Medal of Freedom.

'When someone is cruel or acts like a bully you don't stoop to their level. No, our motto is: when they go low, we go high.'

MICHELLE OBAMA

(born 17 January 1964, USA)

Lawyer and politician

As the first African-American woman to become First Lady of the United States, Michelle Obama showed black women worldwide that they mattered. As herself, she achieved even more.

Growing up in a traditionally working-class household in Chicago, Illinois, Obama worked hard to overcome racial and gender discrimination and achieve success. She graduated from Princeton and Harvard universities and entered a career as a lawyer before meeting her husband, Barack Obama, and campaigning for him to become the forty-fourth President of the United States.

Obama went above and beyond the role of First Lady, becoming a tour de force in her own right through her inspirational speeches. During her time in the White House, she campaigned ardently for women's rights and education. She celebrated being a 'real woman' rather than just an untouchable political figure, appearing on TV chat shows, dancing to hip-hop and becoming a fashion icon by injecting modernity into political style. She even rated as more popular than her husband during his time in office, endearing herself to many through her affable character.

Successful in her career, a devoted mother and an impassioned politician, Michelle Obama is proof that women do not have to restrict themselves to just one box.

'What draws men and women together is
stronger than the brutality and tyranny
which drive them apart.'

MILLICENT FAWCETT

(11 June 1847 – 5 August 1929, UK)

Suffragist

In 1865, nineteen-year-old Millicent Fawcett went to hear MP John Stuart Mill's speech on equal rights for women. She immediately joined his campaign, her first step in a life of suffrage.

A published author and co-founder of a women's college at Cambridge, by her mid-thirties Fawcett had achieved a great deal. When her husband, Henry, died in 1884, she dedicated her life to women's enfranchisement. In 1887, she founded the Liberal Women's Suffrage Society. Ten years later, several suffrage groups merged to become the National Union of Women's Suffrage Societies (NUWSS), with Fawcett as its president. Their non-violent tactics included a protest by 50,000 women in London in July 1913.

The 1918 Representation of the People Act granted property-owning women over thirty the vote. Fawcett retired from the NUWSS, but it wasn't until ten years later that women gained equal voting rights to men, after sixty-three years of campaigning. Fawcett lived to see enfranchisement and died the following year.

In 1925, Fawcett was awarded a GBE and in 1953 the London Society for Women's Suffrage was renamed the Fawcett Society. In 2018, Fawcett became the first woman to have a statue in Parliament Square, a tribute to her lasting impact upon British society.

'What you wear is how you present yourself to the world, especially today, when human contacts are so quick. Fashion is instant language.'

MIUCCIA PRADA

(born 10 May 1949, Italy)

Fashion designer

A PhD in political sciences, mime-artist training and Italian Communist Party membership doesn't sound like a recipe for a fashion designer but that makes Miuccia Prada who she is.

Prada inherited a leather-goods business in 1978, but her first success was a black backpack made from a common nylon traditionally used for parachutes. With only a small triangular label, the utilitarian bag fiercely rejected 1980s ostentation. Not initially well received, it went on to exemplify nineties minimalism and inconspicuous consumption and is now an iconic fashion piece.

Expanding into clothing, Prada's designs focus on ideas instead of beauty, politics instead of trends, often dubbed 'ugly chic'. She designs for the intelligent woman, challenging femininity with atypical colour combinations and left-field historical references. In 1992, she launched the less expensive Miu Miu brand (her childhood nickname) catering for younger buyers. The following year she founded a non-profit organisation for young designers.

From a relatively obscure shop and with no formal design training, Prada has created a fashion powerhouse and billion-pound company with hundreds of stores worldwide. Her cerebral designs reject the sex appeal of womenswear, instead finding elegance in understated glamour, cementing her as one of today's most powerful and empowering designers.

*'I don't see why we women should just
wave our men a proud goodbye and
then knit them balaclavas.'*

NANCY WAKE

(30 August 1912 – 7 August 2011, New Zealand)

Spy

Codenamed 'the White Mouse' for her ability to evade capture, at one point Nancy Wake had a five-million-franc bounty on her head and topped the Gestapo's most wanted list.

As a journalist in the early 1930s, Wake interviewed Adolf Hitler for the *Chicago Tribune*. It was an experience that left her determined to bring down the Nazis. In 1940, aged twenty-eight, she left her cosmopolitan life for France to join the war effort as an ambulance driver, and soon after joined the Resistance. Travelling to London, Wake trained in espionage and joined the clandestine intelligence group Special Operations Executive. In 1944, she led a successful army of 7,000 guerrilla fighters in France against the Germans.

Wake stopped at nothing to quash the Nazis, killing an SS officer with her bare hands, cycling 250 miles in seventy-two hours through enemy territory to recover vital codes and leading an attack on Gestapo headquarters. She became a decorated servicewoman, being awarded nine medals. But sadly, VE-Day was not victorious for Wake. She discovered that her beloved husband had been executed by the Nazis for refusing to give her up.

Wake moved back to Britain in 2001 and died in 2011, aged ninety-eight. A nurse, a journalist, a socialite and a spy, yes. But mouse she was not.

'Energy rightly applied can accomplish
anything.'

NELLIE BLY

(5 May 1864 – 27 January 1922, USA)

Journalist

C ommitted to an insane asylum on New York's infamous Blackwell's Island, living in rat-infested rooms, fed rotten bread and vigorously scrubbed down in daily cold showers, Nellie Bly, nurses confirmed, was growing increasingly mad.

After ten days, she was released. Having been institutionalised after feigning insanity in court, Bly had gone undercover in her first assignment as a journalist in 1887, aged twenty-three. A few days later, she published her withering exposé on the insalubrious conditions, neglect and physical abuse, which prompted a full investigation into the hospital and led to healthcare reforms.

Bly's journalism blew the lid on women's rights, prison conditions and corruption in Mexico. But her intrepid 1889 feat made her name. Determined to emulate Jules Verne's hero of *Around the World in Eighty Days*, Phileas Fogg, she endeavoured to beat his fictional record. Despite her editor's fears that the task was too dangerous for a woman, Bly set sail from New York on 14 November. She circumnavigated the globe in seventy-two days, six hours and eleven minutes, beating Fogg fair and square.

At a time when women's journalism was limited to fluff, Bly's fearless commitment to uncovering the truth helped spearhead undercover journalism. She died, aged fifty-seven, in 1922.

'She was a trained expert in the modern sense – in the sense in which biology has ceased to be a playground for the amateur and a plaything for the mystic.'

NETTIE STEVENS

(7 July 1861 – 4 May 1912, USA)

Geneticist

B efore Nettie Stevens, scientists believed that gender was determined by the mother and her environment. Stevens, though, suspected otherwise. Her work led to one of the most important discoveries in the history of genetics.

Born in Vermont in 1861, Stevens worked as a teacher to save up for her education. Eventually, at thirty-five, she was able to study, earning herself a PhD in biology from Bryn Mawr University in 1903. Receiving a grant to spend a year at the Carnegie Institute of Washington, Stevens began studying mealworms. She noticed that their sperm contained either a large or a small chromosome, while an egg has only large chromosomes. In 1905, Stevens published a paper arguing that the combination of chromosomes determined the gender of offspring and it was therefore the male who determined gender. The discovery was groundbreaking, and formed the basis of the XY chromosome signifiers. But it wasn't until another – male – scientist, Edmund Beecher Wilson, came to the same conclusion that her theory was accepted.

Stevens continued to research for the rest of her life until she died of breast cancer, aged fifty. Her career started late and her life ended early, but she changed the face of science and became one of the first world-renowned female scientists.

'I don't think of myself as a leader, but as part of a chain. If it wasn't for all the amazing women who came before me, I wouldn't be able to do any of it.'

NIMCO ALI AND LEYLA HUSSEIN

(Ali born 1982/1983, Hussein born 1980, Somalia)

Activists

S omalians Nimco Ali and Leyla Hussein grew up in different countries but both underwent the barbaric procedure of female genital mutilation at seven years old. Four years later, complications from Ali's procedure resulted in kidney failure. Hussein suffered panic attacks and blackouts every time she visited the gynaecologist. But both women refuse to be victims. They are survivors of FGM and spend their lives campaigning against it.

Hussein trained as a psychologist, working with young people to raise awareness of gender-based violence. She is a founder of survivor support group The Dahlia Project. Ali is a woman's rights activist and respected writer. In 2010, the women founded the non-profit organization Daughters of Eve. The group aims to protect women in high-risk communities, warn of the danger of FGM and dispel the myth that it is anything other than gender-based child abuse. Despite having the ear of the UK government, both women have suffered vile threats for their work, but bravely continue the fight.

With an estimated 200 million women worldwide living with FGM, their work is not yet done. In 2017, Ali entered politics on behalf of the Women's Equality Party, and both women continue to dedicate their lives to ending the abuse.

*'An artist's duty, as far as I'm concerned, is
to reflect the times.'*

NINA SIMONE

(21 February 1933 – 21 April 2003, USA)

Musician and activist

September 1963 drastically changed the direction of Nina Simone's career. Until then she had sung love songs – but when a bomb dropped by while supermacists hit a church in Birmingham, Alabama, killing four black schoolgirls, civil rights became her *raison d'être*. Channelling her devastation into music, Simone wrote 'Mississippi Goddam', a gut-wrenching call to arms that defined her as a figurehead of the movement.

Simone had played piano in church as a child before dropping out of the Julliard School of Music due to financial limitations and instead performing at local nightclubs. Her deep, resonant voice set her apart and she became known as the 'high priestess of soul'. Her voice embodied the sound of civil rights, singing protest songs that radiated black pride. Aligning herself with Martin Luther King Jr and Malcolm X, she was outspoken in her beliefs, to the detriment of her career. Venues declined her and radio stations refused her music. None of this deterred Simone.

America did though. Fed up with racial hatred, Simone eventually settled in France, suffering with bipolar disorder and hallucinations. She died on 21 April 2003. Having turned her back on a jazz career in favour of political activism, Simone left a legacy exemplifying the political power of music and remains influential in popular culture today.

'My heart will always be in Brixton.'

OLIVE MORRIS

(26 June 1952 – 12 July 1979, UK)

Activist

A young black woman with cropped hair stands barefoot in Brixton's Coldharbour Lane. A cigarette in her right hand, she defiantly holds a placard that reads: 'BLACK SUFFERER FIGHT POLICE PIG BRUTALITY'. The woman is Olive Morris and she is remembered as a community hero.

Born in Jamaica in 1952, Morris moved with her family to south London when she was nine. She left school with no qualifications but in 1977 earned a degree in social sciences at the University of Manchester, where she set up the Black Women's Mutual Aid and the Manchester Black Women's Co-op. Returning to London, Morris founded the Organisation of Women of African and Asian Descent and the Brixton Black Women's Group. She was also a member of the British Black Panthers. A fearless and principled campaigner, Morris wrote of prejudice in local newspapers and was a central figure in the 1970s squatters' campaigns, working to rehouse black families.

At twenty-seven, Morris was diagnosed with cancer and underwent unsuccessful treatment, dying in 1979. Tireless in her fight against prejudice, her short life made an enormous impact. A Brixton council building was named Olive Morris House in 1986. Her face now graces the Brixton £1 note and in 2011 the Olive Morris Memorial Award was set up to provide grants to young black women.

'Think like a queen. A queen is not afraid to fail.
Failure is another stepping stone to greatness.'

OPRAH WINFREY

(born 29 January 1954, USA)

Presentor, actor and philanthropist

To grow up in abject poverty and, through hard work and sheer determination, overcome your lot to reap a fortune is the American dream. And it is personified in Oprah Winfrey.

Born to underprivileged teenage parents on a modest farm in rural Mississippi, as a child Oprah suffered sexual assaults and ran away from home. At fourteen, she fell pregnant but her son died in infancy.

Early in her career, Oprah presented a low-rated Chicago TV show. Within months the show's airtime doubled and its name changed to *The Oprah Winfrey Show*. Oprah's affable personality endeared her to people, encouraging them to open up, and she candidly broached topics never previously discussed on television. It became the highest-rated talk show in history.

The first African-American woman billionaire, a television producer, an Oscar-nominated actor and a lauded author: Oprah's meteoric rise to fame earned her mononym status and the nickname 'queen of all media'. In 2013, she was awarded the Presidential Medal of Freedom. She has donated millions to help women and children and launched her own charities. Oprah's incredible story and her compassionate, philanthropic character make her one of the most influential and admired women today.

'You can decide your own fate. Are you going to let it all fall apart? Or are you going to own it?'

PATTI SMITH

(born 30 December 1946, USA)

Musician and writer

It's February 1971 and a church in New York's Bowery is closed to the congregation; a different kind of preacher has taken to the lectern. A twenty-four-year-old with a shock of unkempt hair reaching to the shoulders of an oversized, boxy blazer reads poetry to the accompaniment of an electric guitar. Andy Warhol and Allen Ginsberg watch Patti Smith's stage debut.

Four years later, Smith recorded one of the most important albums of the twentieth century, *Horses*. The 'godmother of punk', she ushered in a movement that spoke to the youth and disenfranchised alike.

Having grown up in a poor family, Smith dropped out of school and began working in a factory. She fell pregnant at nineteen, but unable to provide for a child, gave it up for adoption. Three months after the birth, in 1967, Smith upped sticks to New York. Surrounded by aspiring artists also living hand-to-mouth in the notorious Chelsea Hotel, she nurtured her love of poetry, publishing three volumes before forming the Patti Smith Group.

Her bestselling 2010 memoir, *Just Kids*, received a National Book Award and her electrifying live performances continue to sell out. Her gender-defying appearance and unique fusion of poetry and punk have cemented Patti Smith as a cultural icon.

*'An apparition, a very wonderful apparition
of how wonderful and expansive life could be.'*

PAULINE BOTY

(6 March 1938 – 1 July 1966, UK)

Artist

L ike many female artists, Pauline Boty fell into obscurity following her death, but she made an invaluable contribution to the canon as the 'First Lady of pop art'. The 1960s art movement was known for being male-dominated and objectifying, pasting passive pin-up girls on enormous canvasses. But Boty, the only female member of the British pop art movement, strived to do the opposite. Her work fiercely rejected the male gaze and boldly addressed women's sexual desires.

At the age of sixteen, Boty won a scholarship to Wimbledon School of Art before going on to the Royal College of Art, where she trained alongside David Hockney and Peter Blake. In 1961, her work appeared in the first-ever pop art exhibition, 'Blake, Boty, Porter, Reeve,' and she was featured in the seminal 1962 documentary *Pop Goes the Easel*.

Alongside her art, Boty boasted acting credits, presented a radio arts show and modelled in *Vogue*. In 1963, she married literary agent Clive Goodwin. Two years later, during a routine pregnancy scan, cancer was discovered. Fearing for her unborn daughter, Boty refused chemotherapy. She died in 1966, just five months after giving birth, aged twenty-eight, her life and legacy cut tragically short. After her death, Boty's work was dismissed as the dabblings of a socialite. Now curators hope to bring her immense talent out of the shadows and onto gallery walls.

'I am not afraid of you. I am not afraid of lies and fiction . . . Nobody can take away my inner freedom.'

PUSSY RIOT

(formed 2011, Russia)

Musicians and activists

P ulling brightly coloured balaclavas over their faces, five women storm Moscow's Christ the Saviour Cathedral. Onlookers are left aghast as the punk band Pussy Riot deliver their obscenity-filled 'Punk Prayer'.

The lyrics attacked the Orthodox Church for supporting President Putin and called on the Virgin Mary to become a feminist. It was February 2012 and the guerrilla performance went viral. A month later, Nadezhda Tolokonnikova (22), Maria Alyokhina (24) and Yekaterina Samutsevich (30) were arrested and charged with 'hooliganism motivated by religious hatred'.

Denied bail, the women were held for six months awaiting trial. In the West, the case garnered enormous media coverage and Pussy Riot became an international *cause célèbre*. They were sentenced to two years in brutal penal colonies. Samutsevich's sentence was later reduced to probation following appeal.

Founded in 2011 as a collective of eleven female artists who sought to progress women's rights and political freedom under Putin's rule, the group has since doubled in size and continues to protest, facing violence and political resistance. A Russian law forbids the distribution of their work. For a performance lasting less than a minute, the impact will last a lifetime, making icons of the women who sang: 'Become a feminist, we pray thee!'

'I try to create strong beautiful spaces in which people can have their spirits lifted.'

REI KAWAKUBO

(born 11 October 1942, Japan)

Fashion designer

Models walk stone-faced down the runway, their clothes twisting around giant growths protruding from their bodies. Hunchbacks and uneven hips jut out of red and blue gingham. This is Rei Kawakubo's 1997 'Body Meets Dress, Dress Meets Body' collection for Comme des Garçons. Kawakubo sought to displace the status quo and challenge traditional ideals of beauty and sexuality.

The self-taught Japanese designer emerged onto the fashion scene in 1969 when she launched Comme des Garçons ('like the boys') after working in a textile factory. Kawakubo's 1981 Paris debut presented all-black deconstructed designs that transcended the body's limitations, rejecting the garish colour and prevailing bodycon styles of the era. It shocked the media, who termed it 'Hiroshima chic', but Kawakubo's influence proved revolutionary. Her hordes of loyal fans became known as 'the crows' for their all-black attire. Proving to have as much business acumen as artistic flair, Kawakubo has created a billion-pound empire as well as launching a magazine and opening Dover Street Market.

In 2017, Kawakubo became the second-ever living designer to be honoured with a retrospective at New York's Metropolitan Museum. A true fashion renegade, Kawakubo offers an alternative to conventional beauty.

*'Science and everyday life cannot
and should not be separated.'*

ROSALIND FRANKLIN

(25 July 1920 – 16 April 1958, UK)

Chemist

The hunt to discover the structure of DNA could be one of history's most appalling tales of skulduggery. To this day, exactly what occurred remains a mystery.

In 1951, after earning a PhD in chemistry from Cambridge University, Rosalind Franklin became a research associate at King's College London. When Franklin arrived at the lab, fellow scientist Maurice Wilkins took her for an assistant instead of his equal, setting the tone for an icy relationship.

Franklin tried novel techniques to photograph DNA in order to determine its structure. Her efforts proved successful, with the final images – in particular 'photo 51' – revealing that DNA was three-dimensional and that there were two different types.

In January 1953, Wilkins revealed 'photo 51' to competitor James Watson, confirming Watson's own theories about DNA structure. In March that year, he and his research partner, Francis Crick, published their findings. The trio won the Nobel Prize in 1962 for the work. By that time, Franklin had died of cancer.

While it is unknown if Wilkins's actions were deliberately underhand, Franklin's crucial role in the understanding of DNA went unacknowledged for years. Today, her pioneering research is rightly recognised for its integral contribution to science.

'The only tired I was, was tired of giving in.'

ROSA PARKS

(4 February 1913 – 24 October 2005, USA)

Activist

On 1 December 1955, forty-two-year-old Rosa Parks boarded a bus in Montgomery, Alabama, and took a seat. As the bus grew more crowded, Parks and other black passengers were asked to give up their seats for white people. Tired of life as a second-class citizen, Parks refused. She was arrested at the scene and charged with violating the laws of segregation.

Parks's plight attracted the attention of Martin Luther King Jr, who mobilised the legendary Montgomery bus boycott. Soon, every black person in town refused to ride the bus in a protest that lasted for 381 days, ending only when the city lifted its segregation laws. This inspired people in states across the South to stage their own boycotts, eventually leading to the abolishment of the Jim Crow laws and the passing of the Civil Rights Act of 1964.

From secretary of the Montgomery chapter of the NAACP to an icon of the civil rights movement and an active member of the Black Power movement, Parks went on to author four books, and in 1996 was awarded the Presidential Medal of Freedom. A statue was erected in Washington in her honour and upon her death in 2005, aged ninety-two, she became the first woman to lie in state at the US Capitol. Though she suffered death threats for much of her life, her small act of defiance on that Montgomery bus lives on beyond a lifetime.

*'Amazing the things you find when you
bother to search for them.'*

SACAGAWEA

(May 1788 – 20 December 1812, USA)

Explorer

Not much is known about the Native American Sacagawea, but it is believed that in 1805, aged sixteen, she set off on a treacherous two-year expedition across North America with over thirty male explorers and her newborn baby in tow.

Born around 1788, Sacagawea, a Shoshone, was kidnapped from her home in the Rocky Mountains by an enemy tribe. Sold to a much older French-Canadian fur trader named Charbonneau, the twelve-year-old girl became his wife. In 1804, Captains Meriwether Lewis and William Clark arrived at her village on their search for new lands. Keen for a native to accompany them, the explorers called upon Sacagawea and her husband. Just two months after giving birth, she set off on the expedition, carrying her new son, Jean Baptiste.

The only woman on the team, Sacagawea proved an invaluable member. Clark noted in his diaries that she foraged for edible plants and bought horses for travel. In one particularly dangerous moment, she saved vital cargo when the team's boat capsized.

For her pivotal role in the expedition she has been posthumously honoured with numerous statues and awards, including that of Honorary Sergeant. The American suffrage movement adopted Sacagawea as their icon for her fearless resolve.

'Although they are
Only breath, words
which I command
are immortal.'

SAPPHO

(*c.* 630 – *c.* 570 BC, Greece)

Poet

S ome muse that Sappho had a husband and daughter and some that she had two or three brothers. Others say she was banished to Sicily for her political views and conflicting accounts of her death include suicide by jumping off a cliff. What is certain is that she was one of the earliest female writers, a celebrated Greek poet so popular she appeared on coins and was carved into statues. Held in high esteem by Plato, she was referred to as 'the Poetess' next to Homer, 'the Poet.'

Born on the island of Lesbos around 630 BC, Sappho most likely died in her fifties, having produced an enormous body of work. Her sensual verse displays a passionate desire for women and embraces female landmarks from puberty to childbirth, making her an early lesbian icon. So powerful was her poetry that the word lesbian is derived from her birthplace and the word 'sapphic', from her name.

Sappho's lyric poetry was written to be performed to music, making her an early singer/songwriter. Unfortunately, her estimated nine poetry anthologies were lost to time. What remain are citations of her work by other scholars, fragments of papyrus and two complete poems. Nonetheless, Sappho is considered a vital influence on modern verse. She is said to have inspired Roman poets and coined phraseology that entered the popular vernacular centuries before Shakespeare did the same.

'The success of every woman should be the
inspiration to another. We should raise
each other up.'

SERENA AND VENUS WILLIAMS

(Serena born 26 September 1981,
Venus born 17 June 1980, USA)

Sports women

The crowd is silent, watching with baited breath as the thwack of a tennis ball rings out against the taut strings of a racket each time the ball is returned across the net. It lands out; a player sinks to the floor in a moment of elation. She has just won the Australian Open and earnt her twenty-third Grand Slam. Crossing the net to congratulate the victor, Venus Williams is met with the ecstatic embrace of her younger sister, Serena.

The Williams sisters have competed their whole lives as the ultimate professional rivals and have come together as undefeated doubles champions, winning eight Olympic Gold medals. In 2002, they occupied the top two spots in the world rankings.

Growing up in the disadvantaged Los Angeles neighbourhood of Compton, the sisters were coached by their father from a young age. Serena is considered the greatest female tennis player of all time – even winning a Grand Slam whilst pregnant. She has long been the world's highest-earning female athlete.

The sisters' exceptional talent and determination have made them hugely popular. They never let their professional rivalry come between them, each supporting the other and conceding defeat gracefully. Their monumental success has made them an inspiration for many.

'One is not born, but rather becomes,

a woman.'

SIMONE DE BEAUVOIR

(9 January 1908 – 14 April 1986, France)

Writer

The woman who acknowledged the idea that gender behaviours are not innate but a social construct, Simone de Beauvoir is considered the harbinger of modern feminism. In her seminal 1,000-page polemic, *The Second Sex*, de Beauvoir slammed the patriarchy, arguing that women needed to emancipate themselves by no longer passively accepting their subordinate roles in society. Now considered a masterpiece, when first published in 1949 it caused uproar and was even banned by the Vatican. Despite the backlash, it was an immediate success, selling 22,000 copies in the first week and establishing de Beauvoir as one of the great modern thinkers.

Raised a strict Catholic, de Beauvoir denounced religion and left home at eighteen to study philosophy at France's esteemed Sorbonne, where she met the young philosopher Jean-Paul Sartre. The pair formed a lifelong relationship and became leaders of existentialist thinking, publishing journals and teaching philosophy. De Beauvoir's activism in the 1960s extended to condemnation of the Vietnam War.

In 1963, Betty Friedan dedicated *The Feminine Mystique* to de Beauvoir, saying that women's lib owed her everything. De Beauvoir died in Paris in 1986, leaving behind a legacy that challenged women's oppression and entirely radicalised traditional views on gender.

'Educate a girl and you educate the whole area . . . You educate the world.'

THERESA KACHINDAMOTO

(born 1958, Malawi)

Chief and activist

Malawi has one of the highest rates of child marriage in the world. In a country that ranks among the world's poorest, many parents find that no longer having to care for a child eases them financially. One woman is not standing for it.

In 2003, Theresa Kachindamoto was called upon by the Dedza District to be the next senior chief and preside over 900,000 people. Reluctantly accepting the position, she donned the traditional beads and leopard print attire and returned to her hometown.

Arriving in the village, Kachindamoto was horrified to find mothers as young as twelve. She called upon the community to pass a law banning marriage under the age of eighteen and to annul existing child marriages, and became known as 'the child marriage terminator'. When four chiefs continued to allow it, she fired them. Kachindamoto faced fierce opposition and death threats but she continued, eventually ending 850 child marriages by 2016 and ensuring that every girl was sent back to school. Where families couldn't afford to educate the girls, she funded their education herself.

And her work isn't done. Kachindamoto has appealed to increase the marriage age to twenty-one and continues to fight for education. UNICEF hopes to extend her methods to other areas, so that girls all over Malawi can live an equal life.

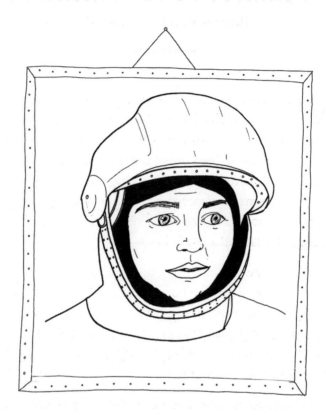

'Hey sky, take off your hat, I'm on my way!'

VALENTINA TERESHKOVA

(born 6 March 1937, Russia)

Cosmonaut

Alone in a spherical vessel, twenty-six-year-old Valentina Tereshkova skyrocketed into space, becoming the first woman in history to do so. It was 16 June 1963, and she orbited the Earth forty-eight times inside the Vostok 6. Upon closing her mission, Tereshkova realised her spacecraft had not been correctly programmed to descend. Immediately contacting ground control, she successfully reprogrammed the system with their guidance. She landed a Soviet hero.

Tereshkova grew up in agricultural surroundings in Russia's Yaroslavl region, leaving school at sixteen to help her mother in a textile factory. In her spare time, she began skydiving and became a regional champion in her early twenties. This passion would help her become one of a handful of women selected to join the Soviet space programme.

It took twenty years before another woman went to space, during which time Tereshkova had become a prominent member of the Communist Party, represented the USSR at the United Nations, headed up the Soviet Women's Committee and raised a daughter. On the fiftieth anniversary of her flight, she was awarded the highest Russian accolade: the Order of Alexander Nevsky.

Today, she remains the only woman ever to go to space solo and the youngest female cosmonaut in history.

'She was the bravest of us all.'

VIOLETTE SZABO

(26 June 1921 – *c.* 5 February 1945, France/UK)

Spy

Violette Szabo faced a Nazi firing squad. She drew her final breath and braced herself as the trigger was pulled.

Szabo had joined the land girls at the outbreak of the Second World War, working in a factory. In 1940, aged nineteen, she met officer Étienne Szabo. They were married within weeks. Szabo quickly fell pregnant, but before Étienne could meet his daughter he was recalled to duty and killed in action. Shortly afterwards, Szabo was contacted by a government espionage agent seeking fluent French-language speakers. Devastated by her husband's death, she agreed to help. This was to be her lover's revenge.

Armed with a secret code in the form of the poem 'The Life That I Have', written by code master Leo Marks for his deceased girlfriend, and with one successful operation under her belt, Szabo headed to France in June 1944. Her mission: to sabotage German communications. But she encountered a German road-block and, unable to flee, provided cover while her comrades escaped. She was captured and tortured by SS officers, but refused to talk. She was executed in 1945, aged twenty-three.

The following year, four-year-old Tania Szabo appeared at Buckingham Palace to collect her mother's posthumously awarded George Cross. Szabo was a true martyr, and her tragic story remains one of the ultimate tales of romance and female resolve.

*'Lock up your libraries if you like; but there
is no gate, no lock, no bolt that you can set
upon the freedom of my mind.'*

VIRGINIA WOOLF

(25 January 1882 – 28 March 1941, UK)

Writer

It was in the spring of 1941 that Virginia Woolf pulled on her overcoat, filled the pockets with handfuls of rocks and walked into the cold, harsh currents of the River Ouse.

Woolf's early life had been punctuated by trauma: she was sexually abused by her half-brothers and lost her mother and sister early. But her intellectual bluestocking background nurtured her early writing. She surrounded herself with free-thinking bohemians – her influential circle of peers, the Bloomsbury Group, became notorious for their sexually liberal, anti-establishment lifestyle. Woolf's own love affair with her friend Vita Sackville-West greatly influenced her work.

It was her unique style of writing that really set Woolf apart. The stream-of-consciousness prose she employed was considered revolutionary, rejecting the traditional novel structure and marking her out as one of the pre-eminent modernist writers. Woolf's books addressed the human condition, grappling with themes of mental health (*Mrs Dalloway*, 1925), homosexuality and gender fluidity (*Orlando*, 1928), and feminism (*A Room of One's Own*, 1929).

Woolf, however, continued to be plagued with depression. As the threat of German invasion loomed over Britain, she took her own life, aged fifty-nine. Today, she is considered one of the most radical writers of the twentieth century and an icon of the feminist movement.

'The only reason I'm in fashion is to destroy the word "conformity".'

VIVIENNE WESTWOOD

(born 8 April 1941, UK)

Fashion designer

Today, London's affluent King's Road doesn't look much like the type of place that could spark a subcultural fashion revolution. But in 1971 a small boutique became the locus of a movement. There, Vivienne Westwood established the aesthetic for the anti-establishment phenomenon punk, later dressing the movement's pivotal band, the Sex Pistols.

In 1981, Westwood presented her first catwalk show, 'The Pirate Collection'. By now punk had developed into post-punk and new wave, and her designs drove the sartorial evolution. The signature Westwood style crystallised in later collections, in which she played with quintessentially British themes. Embracing traditional fabrics, including pinstripe, tartan and tweed, and repurposing eighteenth-century corsetry, Westwood adapted classic tailoring techniques and radically altered them skewing hemlines and leaving garments looking unfinished.

This rebellious core was not confined to the atelier. Along with building a fashion empire, Westwood posed as Margaret Thatcher on the cover of *Rolling Stone*, went knickerless to collect her OBE from the Queen in 1992, and remains a passionate activist. After over four decades in the industry, Westwood is considered the doyenne of British fashion: a fearless, anti-establishment rebel whose unique vision proves the political power of dress.

'It's made to believe
Women are same as Men;
Are you not convinced
Daughters can also be heroic?'

WANG ZHENYI

(1768 – 1797, China)

Astronomer, mathematician, poet

Taking a circular table to represent the Earth, a crystal lamp to symbolise the sun and a mirror as the moon, Wang Zhenyi rotated the imitation celestial objects and discovered how a lunar eclipse could occur. Her resulting article, 'The Explanation of the Lunar Eclipse', radically dispelled the prevailing Chinese theory that it was down to enraged gods.

Zhenyi was born in China's Qing Dynasty and by the age of eighteen had joined a group of female scholars who concealed their knowledge from the government. Zhenyi mastered trigonometry and grasped the importance of making this subject widely accessible. She translated a number of complex mathematical texts and in 1792, aged twenty-four, produced the revolutionary text *The Simple Principles of Calculation*.

Applying her rigorous mathematical training to astronomy, Zhenyi proved to dissenters that the Earth was spherical, and theorised on the number of stars in the sky. She was also a prolific writer, publishing several volumes of poetry. Her poems despaired at the gulf between rich and poor and argued for gender equality – a subversive move for a woman of the time.

Zhenyi's life was cut short at the age of twenty-nine but her unique intelligence, noteworthy rejection of feudal customs and call for equality left a lasting legacy.

'I create art for the healing of all mankind.'

YAYOI KUSAMA

(born 22 March 1929, Japan)

Artist

D ots and flowers flashed in front of her eyes, covering the walls, furniture and her skin. Ten-year-old Yayoi Kusama's hallucinations were so terrifying that she started seeing a psychiatrist. In later life, the same motifs dominated her canvasses. What appeared to be whimsical was in fact an attempt to 'obliterate' the darkness of her mental health. If not for her art, Kusama admits she would have killed herself long ago.

Born in rural Japan in 1929, Kusama studied art before moving to New York, where she began creating her *Infinity Net* paintings. These thirty-foot canvasses covered with loops of white paint led her to fall in with the city's avant-garde art scene. In the 1960s, Kusama grew notorious for her 'happenings' – performance pieces in which she daubed coloured dots all over naked models across the city. With these stunts, Kusama sought to counter the violence of the Vietnam War and upset the status quo.

Despite artistic success, Kusama's psychoses persisted and in 1977 she checked herself into a mental hospital in Japan, where she still resides today. Now in her eighties, she continues to work.

With an oeuvre that spans conceptual installations, performance, monumental sculpture, fashion and even literature, Kusama is Japan's most famous and successful living artist, known affectionately as the 'polka-dot princess'.

'There are 360 degrees, so why stick to one?'

ZAHA HADID

(31 October 1950 – 31 March 2016, Iraq/UK)

Architect

A sharp slab of concrete points towards the sky like a bird in flight, balanced upon several metal spokes rising up through the ground. A magnificent sight, Germany's Vitra Fire Station was Zaha Hadid's first major commission, completed in 1993.

Hadid had previously been known as a 'paper architect', her exquisite designs – considered too radical – never leaving the page. But just over a decade after her fire station, Hadid became the first woman to receive the prestigious Pritzker Architecture prize.

Born in Baghdad in 1950, Hadid moved to London at twenty-two to study architecture. Characterised by dynamic, undulating sculptural forms that reimagined urban landscapes, her avant-garde designs earned her the moniker 'queen of the curve'. Hadid's revolutionary work has been commissioned worldwide, including the 2012 Olympic London Aquatics Centre.

Despite her gender and ethnicity, Hadid dominated an industry overwhelmingly populated by white men, to become a cutting-edge force in global architecture and a dame in 2012. Her flamboyant style and formidable character set her apart. She died in 2016, leaving markers of her determination and talent around the world, jutting from the earth, raising those ceilings high above the ground.

ACKNOWLEDGEMENTS

This beautiful book you hold in your hands would not exist were it not for my brilliant publisher, Christina Demosthenous, who dreamed it up and saw in me the best person to execute it. Thank you for believing in my work and for enduring stream-of-consciousness emails about renegade women and for keeping me within the word count (an impressive feat to say the least). Thanks, too, to Kitty Stogdon for taking us over the finish line.

Thank you to Sasha, the fiercest and most inspiring woman I know. Everything in this book is because of you. Thank you to Nigel for lighting the fire in my belly and teaching me never to accept less. Thank you, Adam and Klaudia, for championing the women of science. And to Milica and Douglas for so much; your guiding light will be with me always.

Thank you to Rebecca Arnold for putting the idea in my head in the first place, to the Society of Authors for supporting writers, Alice for the lovely illustrations, and to everyone who offered up invaluable advice and happily discussed renegade women with me at the pub and via WhatsApp (you know who you are).

Thank you to all the women in this book for doing things without which I would not have been able to write this book at all.

For women to be seen as truly equal, men must support and champion us. Which is why, above all, I'd like to thank Ryan: my muse, my best friend, my love, whose utter faith in me spurs me on daily. Thank you for your unfaltering support – I only hope I can offer the same in return.

SOURCES OF QUOTES

'*That brain of mine is something more than merely mortal; as time will show.*'
Ada Lovelace, in a letter to Charles Babbage (5 July 1843, held in the British Library)

'*My youth, my inexperience, my sex, all conspired against me.*'
Alice Guy-Blaché, *The Memoirs of Alice Guy-Blaché*, translated by Roberta and Simone Blaché, edited by Anthony Slide (Scarecrow Press, 1986)

'*When you find burden in belief or apparel, cast it off.*'
Amelia Bloomer, widely quoted, including at https://bloomingamelias.wordpress.com

'*Women, like men, should try to do the impossible. And when they fail, their failure should be a challenge to others.*'
Amelia Earhart, widely quoted, including at www.ameliaearhart.com/quotes/

'We have no intention of stopping this fight until we have
   eradicated every single remnant of racism in this country.'
Angela Davis, interviewed in *The Black Power Mixtape
   1967–1975* (2011)

'In spite of everything I still believe that people are really good
   at heart.'
Anne Frank, *The Diary of a Young Girl* (Penguin, 1947)

'All women together ought to let flowers fall upon the tomb of
   Aphra Behn . . . for it was she who earned them the right to
   speak their minds.'
Virginia Woolf, *A Room of One's Own* (Hogarth Press, 1929)

'As long as I live I will have control over my being.'
Artemisia Gentileschi, widely quoted, including at http://www.
   artemisia-gentileschi.com/index.shtml

'For the master's tools will never dismantle the master's house.'
Audre Lorde, *Sister Outsider: Essays and Speeches* (Crossing
   Press, 1984)

'I will not have my life narrowed down. I will not bow down to
   somebody else's whim or to someone else's ignorance.'
bell hooks, interviewed by Melvin McLeod with Maya Angelou,
   Shambhala Sun magazine (January 1998)

'We broke through the feminine mystique and women who
   were wives, mothers and housewives began to find
   themselves as people.'
Betty Friedan, interviewed by Robert Scheer, *Los Angeles
   Times* (26 April 1992)

'We have to teach our girls that they can reach as high as
    humanly possible.'
Beyoncé, The Shriver Report (2014)

'I am fighting as an ordinary person for my lost freedom, my
    bruised body, and my outraged daughters.'
Boadicea's words according to Tacitus, *Annals*, Book XIV,
    chapter 35 (1st century AD)

'I am no bird; and no net ensnares me; I am a free human being
    with an independent will.'
Charlotte Brontë, *Jane Eyre* (Smith, Elder & Co. 1847)

'Life isn't about surviving, it's about cramming in as much joy as
    possible.'
Caitlin Moran, interviewed by Kirsty Young, *Desert Island
    Discs*, Radio 4 (22 January 2017)

'We should begin to dream about and plan for a different world.
    A fairer world.'
Chimamanda Ngozi Adichie, TED Talk (December 2012)

'Sports clothes changed our lives because they changed our
    thinking about clothes. Perhaps they, more than anything else,
    made us independent women.'
Claire McCardell, essay in *Sports Illustrated* (1955)

'I will not be triumphed over.'
Cleopatra's words according to Livy, *History of Rome*, Book
    133, fragment 54 (27–9 BC)

'A girl should be two things: who and what she wants.'
Coco Chanel, as quoted in *The Gospel According to Coco Chanel* by Karen Karbo (Morris Publishing Group, 2009)

'We were fighting for ourselves.'
Dagenham striker Sheila Douglass, quoted in 'Did the Dagenham Women's Equal Pay Fight Make a Difference?' by Claire Heald and Caroline McClatchey, www.bbc.co.uk/news/magazine-11420445 (30 September 2010)

'When you realise the value of all life, you dwell less on what is past and concentrate more on the preservation of the future.'
Dian Fossey's final journal entry, as quoted in *Dian Fossey* by Robin S. Doak (Raintree Publishers, 2015)

'Fashion must be the most intoxicating release from the banality of the world.'
Diana Vreeland, *DV* (HarperCollins, 1984)

'I was captured for life by chemistry and by crystals.'
Dorothy Hodgkin, quoted in *Dorothy Hodgkin: A Life* by Georgina Ferry (Granta, 1998)

'I'll see what an ordinary English girl, without credentials or money can accomplish.'
Dorothy Lawrence, *Sapper Dorothy Lawrence* (Lane, 1919)

'Patriotism is not enough. I must have no hatred or bitterness towards anyone.'
Edith Cavell, quoted in *Source Records of the Great War* Vol. III, edited by Charles F. Horne (National Alumni, 1923)

'You can have anything you want in life if you dress for it.'
Edith Head, *How to Dress for Success* (Random House, 1967)

'Trees are not know by their leaves, nor even their blossoms, but
by their fruits.'
Eleanor of Aquitaine, quoted in *Celebrating Motherhood: A
Comforting Companion for Every Expecting Mother,* edited
by Andrea Alban Gosline and Lisa Burnett Bossi (Conari
Press, 2002)

'No one can make you feel inferior without your consent.'
Attributed to Eleanor Roosevelt in *Reader's Digest*
(September 1940)

'Men their rights, and nothing more; women their rights, and
nothing less.'
Elizabeth Cady Stanton and Susan B. Anthony, motto of their
newspaper, *The Revolution*

'Punishment is not for revenge, but to lessen crime and reform
the criminal.'
Elizabeth Fry, from a note found among her papers; Rachel
E. Cresswell and Katherine Fry, *Memoir of the Life of
Elizabeth Fry* (1848)

'Though the sex to which I belong is considered weak you will
nevertheless find me a rock that bends to no wind.'
Elizabeth I, widely quoted, including at http://www.cfwd.org.
uk/quotations-2/elizabeth-I

'I would rather be a rebel than a slave.'
Emmeline Pankhurst, WSPU speech, 14 July 1913, quoted in
   Emmeline Pankhurst: A Biography by June Purvis
   (Routledge, 2002)

'I attribute my success to this – I never gave or took any excuse.'
Florence Nightingale, from a letter of 1861, quoted in *The Life
   of Florence Nightingale* by Sir Edward Cook (Macmillan,
   1913)

*'There is nothing more precious than laughter. It is strength to
   laugh and lose oneself.'*
Frida Kahlo, *The Diary of Frida Kahlo: An Intimate Self-Portrait*
   (Bloomsbury, 1995)

*'You can bind my body, tie my hands, govern my actions: you are
   the strongest, and society adds to your power; but with my
   will, sir, you can do nothing.'*
George Sand, *Indiana* (Michel Lèvy, 1832)

'A woman has two choices: either she's a feminist or a masochist.'
Gloria Steinem, interviewed by Robin Finn, *New York Times* (23
   May 2001)

*'From then on, when anything went wrong with a computer, we
   said it had bugs in it.'*
Grace Hopper, *Time* (16 April 1984)

*'Artists should stop making art only for the 1 per cent and start
   making some art for the rest of us.'*
Guerrilla Girls, *Interview* magazine (23 March 2012)

'There was one of two things I had a right to, liberty, or death; if I could not have one, I would have the other.'

Harriet Tubman, quoted in *Harriet, The Moses of Her People* by Sarah Bradford (Geo. R. Lockwood & Son, 1886)

'I'm a sworn enemy of convention.'

Hedy Lamarr, quoted in *Hedy Lamarr: Her Words* by Ann Kannings (ebook published by Lulu.com, 22 January 2014)

'It is easy to be a bystander and I vowed never to be one.'

Helen Bamber, interviewed by Emine Saner, *Guardian* (8 March 2011)

'Until women were free of the fear of unwanted pregnancy, they would not be able to take up the equal opportunity of work.'

Helen Brook, quoted in her obituary, *Independent* (8 October 1997)

'The best and most beautiful things in the world cannot be seen nor even touched, but just felt in the heart.'

Helen Keller, in a letter to the Reverend Phillips Brooks, 8 June 1891, quoted in *The Story of My Life* by Helen Keller (Doubleday, Page & Co, 1903)

'To all the little girls who are watching this, never doubt that you are valuable and powerful and deserving of every chance and opportunity in the world to pursue and to achieve your own dreams.'

Hillary Clinton, concession speech (9 November 2016)

'I felt that one had better die fighting against injustice than to die like a dog or a rat in a trap.'
Ida B. Wells, *Crusade for Justice* (written in 1928; published by University of Chicago Press in 1970)

'I was brought up to believe that a person must be rescued when drowning, regardless of religion and nationality.'
Irena Sendler, quoted in 'I'm No Hero, Says Woman Who Saved 2,500 Ghetto Children' by Kate Connolly, *Guardian* (15 March 2007)

'Playing lifts you out of yourself into a delirious place.'
Jacqueline du Pré, quoted in *Jacqueline du Pré: Her Life, Her Music, Her Legend* by Elizabeth Wilson (Arcade Publishing, 1998)

'There is a stubbornness about me that never can bear to be frightened at the will of others. My courage always rises at every attempt to intimidate me.'
Jane Austen, *Pride and Prejudice* (Thomas Egerton, 1813)

'We are those lions, Mr Manager.'
Jayaben Desai, quoted in her obituary, *Guardian* (28 December 2010)

'It is impossible to live without failing at something, unless you live so cautiously that you might as well not have lived at all – in which case, you fail by default.'
J. K. Rowling, speech at Harvard (5 June 2008)

'It was for this that I was born!'
Joan of Arc, quoted in *Maid of Heaven: The Story of Saint Joan of Arc* by Ben D. Kennedy (RLK Press, 2007)

'It was a tribute to her ability that her equality with the men was never in question, even in those unenlightened days.'
Michael Smith, *The Bletchley Park Codebreakers* (Biteback, 2011)

'I did take the blows [of life], but I took them with my chin up, in dignity, because I so profoundly love and respect humanity.'
Josephine Baker, quoted in *Josephine Baker: Entertainer* by Alan Schroeder and Heather Lehr Wagner (Chelsea House, 2006)

'If you obey all the rules, you miss all the fun.'
Katharine Hepburn, quoted in an article by Pauline Kael, *New Yorker* (1987)

'I counted everything: the steps, the dishes, the stars in the sky.'
Katherine G. Johnson, quoted at http://thehumancomputerproject.com/women/katherine-johnson

'This is not a story of misery. This is a story of how strong the human mind can be.'
Katie Piper, talk at Stylist Live (18 October 2015)

'If your compliments are making women feel uncomfortable, scared, anxious, annoyed or harassed, you're probably not doing them right.'
Laura Bates, *Stylist* magazine (8 March 2017)

'Naturally I took pictures. What's a girl supposed to do when a battle lands in her lap?'
Lee Miller, radio interview in 1946, quoted in an article by Janine di Giovanni, *New York Times* (21 October 2007)

'There is no such thing as a perfect feminist, and I am no exception.'
Lena Dunham, quoted in an article by Natalie Turco-Williams, *Dazed* magazine (27 April 2015)

'I love physics with all my heart . . . It is a kind of personal love, as one has for a person to whom one is grateful for many things.'
Lise Meitner, in a letter to Elisabeth Schiemann, quoted in *Lise Meitner: A Life in Physics* by Ruth Lewin Sime (University of California Press, 1997)

'They thought that the bullets would silence us, but they failed.'
Malala Yousafzai, UN speech (12 July 2013)

'They just messed with the wrong woman.'
Manal al-Sharif, speech at Oslo Freedom Forum (8 May 2012)

'There was no choice but to be pioneers.'
Margaret Hamilton, quoted in an article by A. J. S. Rayl, NASA, https://www.nasa.gov/50th/50th_magazine/scientists.html

'Nothing in life is to be feared; it is only to be understood.'
Marie Curie, quoted in a speech by Glenn T. Seaborg, *Bulletin of the Atomic Scientists* (January 1968)

'To me, the only sin is mediocrity.'
Martha Graham, *New York Times* (31 March 1985)

The carpenter's daughter has won a name for herself, and has deserved to win it.'
Uncredited author on Mary Anning, in *All the Year Round* periodical, edited by Charles Dickens (1865)

'Fashion is not frivolous. It is a part of being alive today.'
Mary Quant, quoted in *Fashion: The Ultimate Book of Costume and Style* (Dorling Kindersley, 2012)

'The grateful words and smile which rewarded me for binding up a wound or giving a cooling drink was a pleasure worth risking life for at any time.'
Mary Seacole, *Wonderful Adventures of Mrs Seacole in Many Lands* (James Blackwood, 1857)

'Age has not abated my zeal for the emancipation of my sex from the unreasonable prejudice too prevalent in Great Britain against a literary and scientific education for women.'
Mary Somerville, *Personal Recollections of Early Life to Old Age* (John Murray, 1873)

'I do not wish [women] to have power over men; but over themselves.'
Mary Wollstonecraft, *A Vindication of the Rights of Women* (James Moore, 1792)

'Matilda tested the presupposition of male sovereignty, almost to destruction.'
Helen Castor, *She-Wolves: The Women Who Ruled England Before Elizabeth* (Faber & Faber, 2010)

'Human beings should understand how other humans feel no matter where they are, no matter what their language or culture is, no matter their age, and no matter the age in which they live.'
Maya Angelou, interviewed by Alison Beard, *Harvard Business Review* (May 2013)

'When someone is cruel or acts like a bully you don't stoop to
their level. No, our motto is: when they go low, we go high.'
Michelle Obama, speech at the Democratic National
Convention (25 July 2016)

'What draws men and women together is stronger than the
brutality and tyranny which drive them apart.'
Millicent Fawcett, quoted in *Millicent Garratt Fawcett* by Ray
Strachey (John Murray, 1931)

'What you wear is how you present yourself to the world,
especially today, when human contacts are so quick. Fashion
is instant language.'
Miuccia Prada, interviewed by Alessandra Galloni, *Wall Street
Journal* (18 January 2007)

'I don't see why we women should just wave our men a proud
goodbye and then knit them balaclavas.'
Nancy Wake, quoted in her obituary, *New York Times*
(13 August 2011)

'Energy rightly applied can accomplish anything.'
Nellie Bly, quoted in *Eighty Days: Nellie Bly and Elizabeth
Bisland's History-Making Race Around the World* by
Matthew Goodman (Ballantine, 2013)

'She was a trained expert in the modern sense – in the sense in
which biology has ceased to be a playground for the amateur
and a plaything for the mystic.'
Thomas Hunt Morgan, 'The Scientific Work of Miss N. M.
Stevens', *Science*, Vol. 36, No. 928 (October 1912)

'I don't think of myself as a leader, but as part of a chain. If it wasn't for all the amazing women who came before me, I wouldn't be able to do any of it.'

Nimco Ali, 'Think About the Bigger Picture: Life Lessons from Meryl Streep and Other Successful Women', *Guardian* (21 January 2017)

'An artist's duty, as far as I'm concerned, is to reflect the times.'

Nina Simone, interviewed in *Nina Simone: Great Performances – College Concerts and Interviews* (2009)

'My heart will always be in Brixton.'

Olive Morris, quoted at http://brixtonpound.org/docs/ BrixtonPoundUserGuide_FINAL7.pdf

'Think like a queen. A queen is not afraid to fail. Failure is another stepping stone to greatness.'

Oprah Winfrey, widely quoted, including in *Business Insider* (3 November 2014)

'You can decide your own fate. Are you going to let it all fall apart? Or are you going to own it?'

Patti Smith, interviewed by Tim Jonze, *Guardian* (16 June 2016)

'An apparition, a very wonderful apparition of how wonderful and expansive life could be.'

David Alan Mellor, quoted by Ali Smith in 'Ali Smith on the Prime of Pop Artist Pauline Boty', *Guardian* (22 October 2016)

'I am not afraid of you. I am not afraid of lies and fiction . . .
    Nobody can take away my inner freedom.'
Pussy Riot member Maria Alyokhina, in her closing statement
    to the court (8 August 2012)

'I try to create strong beautiful spaces in which people can have
    their spirits lifted.'
Rei Kawakubo, interviewed by Jess Cartner-Morley, *Guardian*
    (5 May 2017)

'Science and everyday life cannot and should not be separated.'
Rosalind Franklin, in a letter to her father, Ellis Franklin (1940)

'The only tired I was, was tired of giving in.'
Rosa Parks, *Rosa Parks: My Story*, with Jim Haskins (Scholastic, 1992)

'Amazing the things you find when you bother to search for them.'
Sacagawea (attributed), widely quoted, including at http://www.
    azquotes.com/quote/772986

'Although they are / Only breath, words / which I command / are
    immortal.'
Sappho, translated by Mary Barnard in *Sappho: A New*
    Translation (University of California Press, 1958)

'The success of every woman should be the inspiration to
    another. We should raise each other up.'
Serena Williams, quoted in *Marie Claire* (11 July 2016)

'One is not born, but rather becomes, a woman.'
Simone de Beauvoir, translated by H. M. Parshley in *The*
    Second Sex (Alfred A. Knopf, 1953)

'Educate a girl and you educate the whole area . . . You educate the world.'
Theresa Kachindamoto, interviewed by Hannah McNeish, ONE.org (7 March 2016)

'Hey sky, take off your hat, I'm on my way!'
Valentina Tereshkova on take-off, quoted at http://www.bbc.co.uk/news/science-environment-34270395

'She was the bravest of us all.'
Odette Churchill GC, fellow SOE agent

'Lock up your libraries if you like; but there is no gate, no lock, no bolt that you can set upon the freedom of my mind.'
Virginia Woolf, A Room of One's Own (Hogarth Press, 1929)

'The only reason I'm in fashion is to destroy the word "conformity".'
Vivienne Westwood, Vivienne Westwood, with Ian Kelly (Macmillan, 2004)

'It's made to believe / Women are same as Men; / Are you not convinced / Daughters can also be heroic?'
Wang Zhenyi, quoted in Notable Women of China: Shang Dynasty to the Early Twentieth Century, edited by Barbara Bennett Peterson (Routledge, 2000)

'I create art for the healing of all mankind.'
Yayoi Kusama, interviewed by Grady T. Turner, BOMB magazine (Winter 1999)

'There are 360 degrees, so why stick to one?'
Zaha Hadid, interviewed by Simon Hattenstone, Guardian (3 February 2003)

A
celebration
of 100
renegade
women